EUROPEAN —
NOT APPLICABLE
TO N. AMERICA

How to Attract Birds to your Garden

Other books by the same author
and published by Robson Books

Times Nature Diary
Feather Report

How to Attract Birds to your Garden

DERWENT MAY

ILLUSTRATED BY PETER BROWN

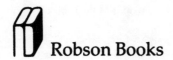

Robson Books

First published in Great Britain in 2001 by Robson Books,
64 Brewery Road, London N7 9NT

A member of the Chrysalis Group plc

British Library Cataloguing in Publication Data
A catalogue record for this title is available from the British Library

ISBN 1 86105 439 4

Typeset by SX Composing DTP, Rayleigh, Essex
Printed in Great Britain by Butler & Tanner Ltd, Frome and London

CONTENTS

Preface

Many readers write to me at *The Times* in response to my weekly column about birds, 'Feather Report'. I have mentioned in this book some of the things they have seen birds doing in their gardens, and should like to thank them for their contributions.

Birds on the Ground

Let us begin at the beginning – the ground. Throwing crumbs on the ground is the simplest and most ancient way of feeding birds, and is still one of the best.

If you do that, house sparrows will be the first birds to come flocking down to the lawn or the paths in your garden – at any rate, in those parts of the country where they are still common. But they are not so widespread as they used to be, when they fed in the roads on the scattered oats from horses' nosebags.

Noisy starlings will bustle up to join the sparrows, a robin may flit down from a fence and a pink-breasted male chaffinch hop shyly up to one of the outer crumbs. Blackbirds – both the glossy black male and the dark brown female – will come swirling in, grab a large piece of bread and go swooping off low over the lawn to the bushes. ('Low-level dive bombers' a boy I knew used to call them.)

It can be a delightful and lively scene, and in a back garden you can often just throw the crumbs out from the kitchen door. But a correspondent of mine on *The Times* told me that his thoughtful old mother always used to say to him 'Don't forget the front'. Birds will come down just as happily to a front garden, or even to the road in front of the house when it is quiet.

Other scraps of unwanted food can be thrown out as well as crumbs. Many garden birds like cooked potatoes – mashed or boiled. Cooked rice and pasta are fine – but not uncooked rice grains, which can swell up in a bird's stomach. Squashy apples are popular. Robins like cheese, especially grated cheese, if its flavour is not too strong.

It is a good idea to scatter small portions of the food, so that more birds have a chance of getting something. There will be also be less quarrelling among them. Some people even put a fine wire mesh over pieces of bread on the lawn so that larger birds cannot take too much at a time, or carry big pieces off. Dry bread should be well moistened and broken up so that it is easier to eat. The large, hard end of an old French baguette will not go down well.

Bacon rind is popular, provided the bacon is not too salty. Avoid any very salty food that birds might eat without realising that it is dangerous for them. Some years ago, hundreds of dead bramblings – a colourful relative of the chaffinch that comes here in winter from Scandinavia – were found dead on a roadside. They had been drinking water contaminated by salt that the local council had put down on the icy road.

Water

The other important way in which the ground can be used is to put out water for drinking and bathing. Birds can be in serious need of water both in the summer when it is very hot, and in the winter when puddles and ponds are frozen. They will eat snow, but they lose precious warmth and energy when they do. A bowl of water will always attract them.

It should be near bushes or trees, because birds are nervous when they come down to wash or drink, and they like to have a refuge nearby to retreat to if they are startled. Also, birds with wet feathers cannot fly so well and need a safe place at hand to dry out. But do not put the bowl too close to any kind of cover that might be a good hiding-place for a cat.

It is a pleasure to watch birds coping with water. Small birds drink it by sipping the water, then throwing their head back to swallow it. One needs to make sure that the water level is high enough for them to lean over and reach it from the brim. Among British birds, only the pigeons can suck water up through their beaks without raising their heads.

Bathing birds are a dramatic sight. A blackbird, for instance, will stand in the water, lean forward and dip into it, then jerk back and jerk its wings up at the same time so that water is sprinkled all over it. Birds' feathers can get sticky, which spoils the seamless coat of feathers that they need to keep them warm, and can also make it harder for them to fly. They frequently preen their feathers with their beaks, but sometimes they feel the need for a good wash. However, a large bird like a blackbird can quickly empty a bowl in this way, so regular re-filling is required.

A pond will be very popular with birds, provided they can get to the edge of it easily. But the best way of providing water for birds is a birdbath raised off the ground. Birds will be safest there. If it can be kept permanently full, with water flowing into it by some unobtrusive means that will not disturb the birds, that will be best of all.

An old-fashioned bird bath on an ornamental pillar looks attractive, but specialist shops can provide variations such as ceramic dishes on a stand with two compartments, one for shallow and one for deep water, or bird baths that can be hung from the branch of a tree.

Troublemakers

Cats are the great enemies of birds feeding on the ground. Many a bird that has been lured to a scrap of loaf by a bird-lover has met its end in the claws of the bird-lover's own tabby. It is a fate some birds are almost bound to meet as long as cats are kept as pets.

Nevertheless, if one is feeding birds in the garden, one should do all one can to keep them safe. The main thing here is what I said above about bowls of water – do not attract birds down to places on the ground where a cat can easily stalk them and pounce on them.

Other troublemakers on the ground are large birds. Three kinds of pigeon may come down even into quite small gardens – domestic pigeons that are living wild (or feral pigeons, as they are often called), woodpigeons, which are the big, clumsy ones with a white patch on their necks and white wing-bars, and collared doves.

The collared doves are a remarkable species. They were unknown in Britain until the 1950s. In that decade they spread across Europe from their original home in the Balkans, and now they are common in practically every corner of the land. They are small, vivacious pigeons with a dark mark on their long, elastic-looking neck, and a 'coo-COO-coo' song that is sometimes mistaken for the cry of a cuckoo.

The pigeons do not harm the small birds, but they are big bullies with large appetites, and they simply hog the food that has been put out. Sparrows, starlings and blackbirds may nip in among the pigeons and pick up a morsel, but shyer birds are frightened off by them. Even the nimble ones get less to eat when the pigeons are there.

It might be asked 'Why shouldn't the pigeons be fed? After all, they're birds too' – and of course that is a perfectly legitimate point of view. But most people really want to see and to help the smaller birds, and the fact is that the pigeons can normally fend for themselves without these supplements to their diet. I suspect that the decline in the house sparrow population is due in part to increased numbers of pigeons picking up the food that gets dropped on the roads.

Nevertheless, there is no obvious answer to what to do about the pigeons if they come into your garden and you don't want them. To be realistic, the only thing seems to be just to shoo them away, and hope the small birds come back for the crumbs quicker than the pigeons do.

The black birds of the crow family – carrion crows, rooks and jackdaws, who are always on the lookout for easy food – are less likely to come into a small garden, and though you may see jays – which are also crows – they do not often come and feed among small birds. However, magpies – the cheekiest members of the crow family – may come hopping up to take a piece of bread when the coast seems clear. Black-headed and herring gulls may swoop down and carry off food sometimes – I have heard them called 'big white sparrows'.

I shall say more about sparrowhawks when we come to bird tables, but I should mention here that several people wrote to me at *The Times* describing a rather unusual form of behaviour for them. They lurked under bushes and suddenly flew out to pick up an unsuspecting starling or sparrow. In fact, they were behaving more like a cat than a sparrowhawk. However, I don't think they constitute a very serious hazard for birds feeding on the ground.

Last thoughts about the ground

Blackbirds, song thrushes and robins – and even the large mistle thrushes which show silver under their wings when they fly – may all come on to a lawn at any time of the year in search of earthworms and other creatures. They are predominantly ground feeders. But when the earth is frozen hard or covered with snow they find it particularly difficult to get the food that they need.

They go searching under hedges and bushes where the snow may not be so deep, or where there are dry fallen leaves that they can turn over in the hope of finding spiders and insects. When a blackbird is tossing the leaves up vigorously with its beak on a winter's day, you can hear the noise from a long way off.

Such birds will benefit particularly in winter from any food you throw down on the lawn or the paths. Raisins and sultanas will prove very popular with blackbirds and song thrushes: you can buy special packets of them for birds (not for human consumption). You may get quite a flock of quarrelling blackbirds, some of them perhaps winter-visitors, which come to Britain from as far away as Germany or Poland.

Robins, however, are among the few species that occupy and defend a territory in the winter, so you will probably get only one of those – the one that, in the robin's view of the matter, owns your garden, and who will probably be a familiar individual to you. It will be joined by a mate in the spring.

In very harsh weather, food on the ground may even attract a red-wing, a small thrush with a red flash under its wings that comes here for the winter from its northern breeding grounds. Redwings are particularly attracted by apples in a garden.

But there are also shyer birds that forage all the year round under the hedges and bushes, and you may like to help those as well, especially in winter, when they too find the living less easy.

One ground feeder that never ventures far from shelter is the hedge sparrow, or dunnock. When it is looking for food it creeps about on the ground near the hedges and bushes like a mouse, on tiny pink feet. Incidentally it is not a real sparrow – it just got its name because it looks at a glance rather like a female house sparrow. But sparrows are mainly seed-eaters, with stout beaks like the finches to which they are related, whereas the dunnock has a fine, sharp bill, and in the summer feeds mostly on insects. (In winter it takes what it can get.)

Then there are the tiny wrens, which are always whirring like large moths through the undergrowth. They rarely emerge from cover to feed, but they often come down to the tangle of twigs and dead leaves in the hedge-bottoms.

Both these species can be helped by scattering food beneath the bushes and hedges. You may not see them outside your window, but you will get many a glimpse of them when you walk in the garden, and you will hear the extraordinarily loud, rich song of the wren from its hidden perch from early in the spring until late in the autumn. If you manage to see a wren singing – and they come up higher in the branches in March and April – you will find that its whole body vibrates as it launches its rapturous notes on the world.

One final point about food on the ground. It is best to look round the garden in the evening and pick up any food that has been left. It is probably food that the birds do not like, and if it is left out it may attract rats in the night. Don't throw the dinner scraps out tonight – keep them for tomorrow morning!

CHAPTER TWO

The Dangling Peanut

Birds that feed on the ground are not the only birds that come into gardens. One family that normally stays higher up is the titmouse or tit family. Great tits will feed on beech nuts lying under the trees in the woods in autumn and winter, but they do not often come down to the ground in gardens. The smaller tits – the blue tits, coal tits and long-tailed tits – remain well above the earth most of the time.

So they must be attracted to food that is placed higher up. That means either bird tables, or a device that is widely used now, the hanging dispenser or feeder. The two can often be used successfully together.

There are two main kinds of feeder – those that dispense peanuts, and those that dispense seeds. The peanut feeders are made of metal or sometimes of plastic mesh, and the birds hang on the mesh and peck at the peanuts in them through the gaps. The seed feeders are solid tubes, usually made of strong, transparent plastic, with holes in them called portholes or ports through which the birds can get at the seeds inside. There is generally a well-placed perch or set of perches for the birds to sit on while feeding at the ports. Both kinds of feeder have a solid base, and a lid or roof on top. These fittings may be made either of metal or of plastic.

Peanut feeders

Peanut feeders come nowadays in various forms and sizes. You can of course simply hang up a plastic mesh bag of peanuts. (A string bag is not a very good idea because birds can get their claws caught in it.) Other basic peanut feeders are a simple wire or plastic mesh basket, say six inches long, with a lid on top, or a shallow wooden box with wire mesh at the front. You can buy these very cheaply, or even make one for yourself. Put the peanuts in, hang the feeder up, and leave the birds to it!

But more elaborate ones are also available. Usually these are carefully constructed tubes of stainless steel mesh, sometimes with perches fitted to them. The gaps in the mesh are wide enough for the birds to insert their beaks without damage, but small enough for the peanuts not to fall out.

These feeders can be up to 12 or 15 inches long from top to bottom, but are usually not more than that. If they were longer, the weight of the peanuts when they were full might make them hard to manage, and they might also fall down more easily. With these feeders, as with the simpler ones, you just pour the peanuts in from the top.

Squirrels are the most serious raiders of garden bird-feeders. Feeders that are made entirely of metal resist their assaults most efficiently, and are really the best if you have squirrels in your garden, but of course they are more expensive than plastic feeders or feeders with plastic fittings.

You can also get protection from squirrels with a cage that is fitted round the tube. These cages come in the shape of domes or globes made of steel bars, with the gaps between the bars large enough for the birds to get through and reach the tube inside, while squirrels are kept out – except for an occasional, slim young one! Some of these fortified feeders are designed to look rather beautiful, with a pewter finish and a decorative hanging bracket at the top.

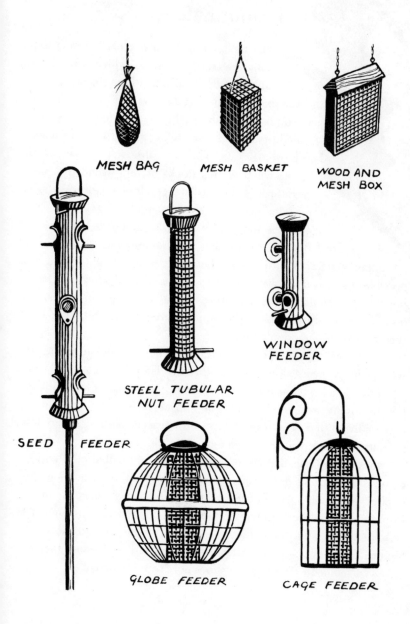

MESH BAG

MESH BASKET

WOOD AND MESH BOX

STEEL TUBULAR NUT FEEDER

WINDOW FEEDER

SEED FEEDER

GLOBE FEEDER

CAGE FEEDER

Peanut Eaters

The tit family particularly like peanuts, especially the sturdy great tit, which is the largest member of the family. But blue tits and coal tits also come to peanut feeders, and sometimes the uncommon marsh tit. In the last few years, long-tailed tits have also started coming to peanut feeders all over Britain. This was almost unknown in the past, when winter flocks of long-tailed tits would pass through the garden trees, looking for insects, but never condescend to take human offerings.

Why the long-tailed tits have descended *en masse* on garden feeders is not known. Their numbers – unlike that of many species of bird – have been increasing recently, and it is possible that this has obliged them to seek new food supplies. Or just possibly the feeders were discovered by a few long-tailed tits, and others saw them hanging there and imitated them, until the habit spread through the population.

At any rate, they will sometimes hang there now, pecking at the nuts with their tiny beaks alongside the other tits. They can even hang by one leg and hold a bit of peanut in the other, pecking smaller bits off it. All the tit family are good at hanging upside down, which they do repeatedly as they search in the trees for insects. Although they love peanuts, they are primarily insect eaters in the summer.

Many other birds that are basically seed eaters will also, of course, come to the peanut dispensers. These are mainly the finches – greenfinches, goldfinches, chaffinches and the little green siskins that emerge from the spruce forests in winter. Goldfinches and siskins are almost as agile as the tits, and greenfinches easily cling sideways to the mesh. Siskins, oddly enough, are particularly attracted by feeders that are coloured red. Otherwise, colour does not seem important.

Peanuts

It is best to supply peanuts to birds in a feeder, because there is always a danger of them choking on a whole peanut if the nuts are just scattered on the ground or put on a bird table. This is particularly important in summer, when birds might be tempted to take a whole peanut and stuff it down the scraggy neck of one of their nestlings.

There are other dangers with peanuts that must be looked out for. Never put out salted peanuts, for the reason I gave above for not putting out salty bacon. You might kill your birds.

They can also be killed by poisoned peanuts. There is a fungus that affects peanuts by producing aflatoxin in them – a tasteless and colourless substance that is generally fatal to birds, attacking their livers and immune systems. The Birdfood Standards Association, which is supported by the wild birdfood trade, the Royal Society for the Protection of Birds and the British Trust for Ornithology, has recently tried to outlaw these dangerous peanuts. As a result, most peanuts sold by regular bird food suppliers are now safe. But it is best to enquire and get an assurance on this point. A certificate of independent testing in the UK should be available.

In general, peanuts are a good bird food because they contain plenty of oil and protein. You can get them in large or standard size – the large ones provide a slightly higher proportion of calories. And if you are lucky, they will attract crowds of birds to your garden.

Seed feeders

These are also long tubes, as described above, with portholes and perches for the birds to get at the seeds inside. They can be much longer than the peanut feeders, because the seeds are lighter then the peanuts. You can buy extraordinary, four-foot-long seed feeders, with as many as 12 portholes, and it is wonderful to see a whole flock of greenfinches or goldfinches perched on them. Some of the seed that they pull out will always spill to the ground, and some of the birds will fly down to the ground to feed there and then fly up again, with a constant flashing of gold wings in both of these species.

In the best of these seed feeders, the tubes are made of a sun-resistant, glass-fibre plastic. The portholes are designed with a metal lip so that water does not get in, and the base of the tube is cup-shaped inside, so that all the seed drops to the bottom and does not lurk in corners where it might get rotten. There is generally a port, or a pair of ports, at the bottom so that the birds can get down to the lowest grains. If there is a tray underneath to catch spilt seeds, that will also be used by the birds. Seed feeders, like peanut feeders, are available in wire cages or 'forts' to stop squirrels getting at them.

Seeds are best fed to birds in dispensers such as these because many get wasted if they are just thrown on the ground. However, there is no reason why you should not do that if you want to.

Seeds

So what kinds of seed should you put in your feeder? Nowadays, a great variety of seeds and grains is available.

Sunflower seeds are the most popular, especially with the finches, and are rich in proteins, oils and minerals.

You can get either plain sunflower seeds, or black sunflower (sometimes called 'oil' sunflower) seeds, which some birds like for their softer flesh, but may be less attractive to garden owners because of the mess of black husks that they leave behind.

You can also get sunflower hearts, which have had the husks removed and provide maximum energy with minimum waste, but which are naturally more expensive. Thrown on the ground, sunflower hearts will attract hedgehogs at night. One problem with them in feeders is that they get sticky when the air is damp, but they can easily be loosened and run freely again if the tube is shaken.

Nyjer (or niger) seed is a small black seed that is sometimes sold as 'thistle seed', though in fact it comes from a kind of Indian daisy that is closely related to sunflowers. Goldfinches love it, and it is possible to buy special nyjer feeders with the size of the porthole adapted to the size of the seeds and the size of the goldfinches' beaks. It has been nick-named 'goldfinch magnet'.

Any of these seeds can be used on their own in feeders, but nowadays it is more usual to offer birds a mix of seeds. Other items that can be mixed with those we have just mentioned are peanut granules, which are the nutritious bits of the peanuts where they germinate; pin-head oatmeal, which is chopped-up oats with the husks taken off – as found on human breakfast tables and hulled millet, another grain, also with the outer coat removed. These are perfectly all right in mixes, but, unlike the sunflower seeds, they do not flow very well if put in seed feeders on their own.

Hemp seeds are added to some mixes. Great tits like them and they also attract nuthatches, which are birds of the treetops that can walk underneath a branch, or up and down a tree-trunk, without any prob-lem. The tits and nuthatches crack the hemp seeds open with their beaks.

A little grit from oystershells is also added sometimes to a mix to provide calcium. This is especially helpful to female birds in the spring when they need a lot of calcium in order to produce strong eggshells. Calcium also helps digestion in birds.

You can buy seed in bulk, or try out small quantities to see what your birds like best, and what kinds of seed attract different species. All the agile birds will come to seed feeders, and sometimes some clumsy ones too, such as an ambitious starling! In general, though, once you have started feeding certain kinds of bird, it is best to keep going with them, since they may have decided to base their territories on your garden, and find it difficult to move elsewhere if you stop. You can always add new feeders, and experiment with other methods, to try to increase the number of species you get.

Other feeders

If you live in a flat, you can still attract birds to your window. You will probably get a few bird visitors if you just put food outside on the window sill, but you can also get various attachments for the window that will bring more along. These include tubular window feeders, both for peanuts and seeds, that are attached by strong suction cups to the window pane. They are basically made in the same way as the other feeders, but are not usually very large or heavy. They provide close-up views of birds, which do not seem to be troubled by shadowy human forms moving about slowly and quietly behind the window.

There are also various kinds of seed tray with one-way mirrored panels behind them for looking at birds through a window. These can be placed on an outside window sill, or attached by suction to the window itself.

One manufacturer offers a very cheap way of getting a hanging feeder. He sells a framework into which you can fit an upside-down mineral water bottle, from which the seeds spill out on to a tray where birds can perch. Anything to have a blue tit in the garden!

Last thoughts on feeders

Although feeders are usually hung from above, they can alternatively be sited on the top of a pole, and specially made poles can be bought from specialist suppliers.

It is important to keep feeders clean. Birds leave a lot of mess behind them, and other birds can sometimes pick up salmonella from it. So take your feeders to pieces regularly – it is easily done – and scrub them with a weak solution of some detergent or disinfectant such as Jeyes Fluid, or the special disinfectant preparations you can buy from bird food suppliers. Take care to wash off all the disinfectant afterwards. And if you make your own wire peanut feeder, use rustproof wire.

One other word of warning – about yourself! Do not hang feeders at that curious and deadly height just above eye-level where it is easy not to notice things. Many an unsuspecting visitor to a garden has got a nasty knock on the head from a hanging feeder, and has cursed the wretched birds – and sometimes even the owner forgets that it is there, and nurses a cut on the forehead as a return for his kindness.

CHAPTER THREE

A Table for the Birds

The bird table is the basic piece of garden furniture for attracting birds, and the one that most people want. Nearly every kind of bird in the garden will come to it at one time or another – the blackbirds, thrushes and robins that are predominantly ground feeders, the tits and finches that mostly live higher up, and even shy birds from the woods such as blackcaps, which belong to the warbler family, and great spotted woodpeckers in their striking black, white and red plumage.

The elements of a bird table

Basically, a bird table is a flat piece of wood on a pole. You can easily make one yourself. But, as with most courtships, there are a number of things to take into account if you want your courtship of the birds to be a success.

The table top should be made of wood that will not warp, and should be fairly large – say 18 to 24 inches by 12 to 18 inches. There is some evidence that, if a bird table gets too crowded, the stress of competing and quarrelling can reduce the birds' immunity, and they can pick up diseases from each other. They are less likely to do that on a large table top. But the larger it is, the more important it is to have it

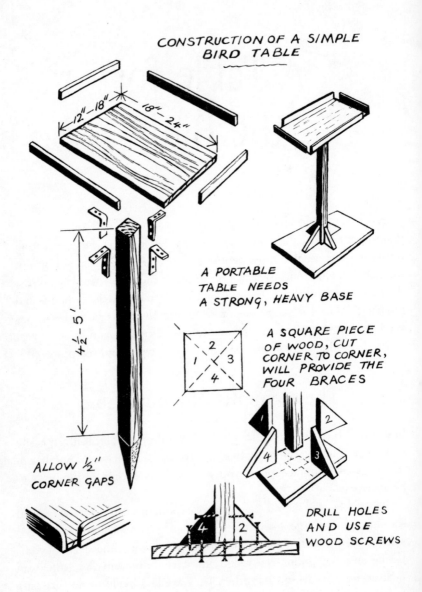

CONSTRUCTION OF A SIMPLE
BIRD TABLE

12" – 18"

18" – 24"

A PORTABLE
TABLE NEEDS
A STRONG, HEAVY BASE

4½ – 5'

A SQUARE PIECE
OF WOOD, CUT
CORNER TO CORNER,
WILL PROVIDE THE
FOUR BRACES

1 2 3 4

ALLOW ½"
CORNER GAPS

DRILL HOLES
AND USE
WOOD SCREWS

securely attached to its pole, and the pole itself well planted in the ground. You don't want it to collapse as soon as a great spotted woodpecker lands on it.

The top should have a low rim stuck or nailed round it from below to stop the food getting knocked off by clumsy birds. There needs to be a gap in the rim at each corner, so that rain will run off more easily, and also so that it is easier to clean and dry the table. The rim can simply be made from four narrow strips of wood cut to size. Make sure that there are no sharp edges left anywhere on the table top, and coat it with a good wood preservative. Plenty of rain is sure to fall on it.

The pole can be of wood or metal and can really be of any height, depending on your preference. For instance, you may want to to be able to see the birds easily through the window when you are sitting down at your own table, and that may determine the best height for it.

However, it is best to have the table top low enough for you to be able to put the food on it without any strain, while high enough to prevent cats easily leaping up onto it. A table top between four-and-a-half and five feet from the ground would probably be best for most people.

The pole must be sturdy. A wooden pole can be attached to the table top by nailing blocks of wood under the table top and then driving screws through these into the pole. Alternatively, using either a wooden or a metal pole, you can nail a single block of wood with a hole in it on to the underside, and fix the pole firmly into this. It is best to add four brackets, either of wood or metal, underneath the table top, to hold it all together more soundly.

The bottom of the pole needs equally careful attention. Drive it firmly into the ground, and consider adding side struts and a base for greater security. If you cannot have a pole that is planted in the ground, make sure you have a heavy, broad, very stable base, with stones piled on it if necessary. A strong wind can send a bird table flying.

These are all points that you should likewise look out for if you are buying a bird table, which is what most people do these days. You can get them from garden centres or from specialist suppliers. Some tables are already made up, others come in parts that you have to assemble yourself. With the latter, it is best to study carefully what it will eventually consist of and look like before you buy it.

Rustic-looking bird tables are pretty, but may not be very efficient. Sometimes they are made of attractive silver birch logs – but those will be quick to rot. Others have quaint, knobbly poles – an open invitation to squirrels and cats to start climbing.

And where should you put your bird table when you have got it? You will almost certainly want to be able to watch it from somewhere in the house, and that will be your first consideration. But again, if you are to attract the birds, there are other things to take into account.

Birds are very exposed on a table, and they like to have somewhere to flee to for cover if they are startled. So the table should be sited fairly near some bushes or trees that they can take refuge in. They also like to use these as a staging point when they are approaching the table. A fence may be enough.

However (there are lots of 'howevers' in this game) the table should not be so close to the trees or bushes that a cat or squirrel can lurk in them, and then jump on to it to snatch up either a feeding bird or the food itself. Safety for the birds must always be one's watchword.

Improving the bird table

There are many additions you can make to a bird table or buy with it, so that it is safer or more attractive.

One possibility is a roof. Many bird tables in garden centres come with a roof, and it is not difficult to add one oneself. But are they a good idea?

Their chief merit is that they keep rain or snow off the food – and off the birds too, though that does not seem to be so important to them. Blackbirds and thrushes will cheerfully feed in the rain, when earthworms come wriggling to the top of the lawn. Roofs also keep large birds such as woodpigeons off the bird table, and are a defence against any sparrowhawks that might swoop down. Large rounded plastic roofs may help to keep off leaping squirrels – which we shall return to in a moment.

On the other hand, birds like to be able to see all round them. With an eye on each side of their head, they are good at that, but they often feel uneasy in a situation where they cannot see the sky or fly upwards immediately they spot danger. So shyer birds are reluctant to come under a roof. If you nevertheless decide on having a roofed bird table, make sure the roof is shaped so that rainwater runs off it and does not flow on to the table.

A more recent invention is the 'squirrel baffle'. In many gardens squirrels are the biggest problem if you want to feed the birds. They are masters at climbing or jumping on to bird tables and taking the food. They will not be able to leap on to the table if it is far enough away from trees and bushes, or fences and walls, but it is astonishing how skilful they are at climbing the poles of bird tables and scrambling on to the top.

The squirrel baffle is a device to stop them from climbing the pole. It may be any improvised kind of disc or block fixed round the pole that they find it hard to get past when they start climbing the pole from the ground. An elementary squirrel baffle can be made out of an upside-down biscuit tin. There are also more sophisticated models designed by specialist firms. These are made of slippery material and are specially shaped to bar the way. But some squirrels, it would seem, are never baffled.

Bird tables — or feeding trays, as they should perhaps then be called — can of course also be hung from branches or lines. That is one way, at any rate, of stopping squirrels climbing up to them.

You can add feeders to a bird table. You can hang them from the sides of the table top, and from the roof, and some people's bird tables look like Christmas trees with so many colourful objects dangling round them. Really, it is best not to overdo it, or you will have too many birds disturbing each other and bickering with each other all the time. Small birds need a steady intake of food, and especially on short winter days they cannot afford to waste too much time.

You can also put a water dish on a bird table, but that too can be more trouble to the birds than it is worth, with water getting spilt and making a mess of the bread. Some manufactured bird tables have a tray made of finely perforated metal so that any water drips through. The tray can also have an unbroken rim around it, so less food falls off.

A nest box is sometimes built in the roof of the table, but this is one of the worst ideas of all. It is most unlikely that any bird will try to breed in it with all the commotion going on below, and if, say, a blue or great tit does try to make its nest there, there will be constant quarrels with other tits that try to come to the table.

Finally, as with the feeders, always keep the bird table clean. It needs regular scrubbing and disinfecting in just the same way as the feeders do.

And now, the menu

So your bird table is in place — out of danger from attacks by cats, rats or squirrels, but easy for the birds to approach, and giving you a good view of its visitors. Now, what to put on it?

All the household scraps mentioned in Chapter One can go there, just as well as on the ground. Bread, cooked rice, cheese, discarded bits of fruit — they will all find a welcome from most species of garden bird. Again, avoid very salty bacon and uncooked rice grains (or pasta sticks). Also remove any wet bread before it goes mouldy — some moulds can be fatal to birds if they breathe them in.

Whole peanuts, as has been said, should not be put on the bird table in case birds choke when they are trying to swallow one. Keep them for putting in the feeders. But all the seeds described in Chapter Two can be put on the bird table and will be gobbled up by the birds.

There is also a range of cereals that are not usually put into seed feeders, either on their own or in mixes, because they flow slowly and can clog up the portholes. These are the grains of wheat, maize, oats and barley. But they are popular with the birds and can be bought either mixed with each other or mixed with the smaller seeds, and are ideal either for putting on the bird table or scattering on the ground. Because they are relatively hard grains, specially softened mixes of them are also available, sometimes mixed with sultanas — a breakfast muesli for blackbirds, song thrushes and robins. Birds are very well catered for nowadays!

One item that has not been mentioned yet is fat. This is popular with birds. Not so many people have dripping or suet left over from their cooking nowadays, but if you have any kind of soft fat that will solidify you can make good use of it.

You can just put lumps of it on the bird table. But you can also make something more interesting. Melt it down in a saucepan, and then stir in almost anything else that birds like – seeds, peanuts, bits of cheese or meat. Then you can pour it into a tin or half a coconut shell and hang that up when the fat has solidified. It can be solidified in the refrigerator, if necessary. You can also buy something called a tit bell, which is a bell made of terracotta that can be turned upside down and filled with your fat mixture. Hang it up like a bell, and the tits will cling to the bottom rim to get at the contents.

It is also possible simply to put a piece of wire through the hardened mixture and just hang it up without a container. And you can buy ready-made bars or cakes of fat, filled with seeds or peanuts. Some of these ready-made bars also contain insects as well to give a richly varied feed.

Now we have come to insects, we can broach what some garden-owners might find a less attractive subject – putting out live food for the birds. Most birds eat insects – flies, caterpillars or worms – as a substantial part of their diet, and even seed-eaters such as greenfinches need to give insects to their young when they are feeding them in the nest. So there is nothing unnatural about feeding them to birds on your bird table. In fact, especially in the breeding season they can be very helpful to parent birds working hard to fill five or six hungry little beaks.

If you want to add live insects to your menu for the birds, you will find them available from various suppliers. The most commonly used are mealworms, which are the larvae or caterpillars of the meal beetle. They come in plastic containers, and should be put into tubs or bowls full of bran or mealworm food for them to eat – since they too must be fed if they are to stay alive!

Then they should be put out in small bowls, also with bran in them, on the bird table. Robins are the birds that are really keen on mealworms, but tits and sparrows and other birds will also readily come for them. They may even tempt down a spotted flycatcher, which normally catches flying insects in the air.

They are also a good food for putting under hedges to help the wrens, which like to forage there as mentioned in Chapter One. It has been observed that wrens will come more readily if you reduce the size of the top of the bowl by putting a log or something of the sort across it. Wrens like the feeling of being hidden.

You will need to clean the bottom of the bowl each time you put new supplies in, because the mealworms leave a residue. You can also buy hanging trays to put mealworms on.

Other worms available include waxworms, the larvae of the wax moth, which do not need to be fed, and earthworms, which are a natural food of blackbirds, song thrushes and robins.

The birds you will see

So what are the birds you are likely to attract to your garden with your crumbs, feeders and bird tables? Here is a short survey of the species you may see, and what they most like to feed on.

Sparrows

There are two kinds of sparrow in Britain. The house sparrow and the tree sparrow. House sparrows were once so common that people scarcely noticed them. Now they have become quite uncommon in some places, especially in the cities where they used to thrive. The males and females are different. The males are very attractive birds, with a grey cap, a large black bib and a jaunty manner. The females are duller birds, with pale brown bodies and darker wings.

They are natural seed-eaters, related to the finches, so they have stout beaks. In autumn, before the days of the combine harvester, they used to go like holidaymakers to the cornfields to eat the grain that was drying in the stooks (which were like little tents made of sheaves). But they also eat insects, often flying out and trying to snap up flies on the wing.

They will feed on almost anything you put out, either on the ground or on the bird table, but they are not so acrobatic as some of the other birds and are not seen so much on feeders. They sometimes sit in the trees and bushes round a table, waiting nervously to come down; then one, braver than the others, flies down, and the others immediately follow him.

Tree sparrows are smaller, shyer birds, and are now very uncommon, but they may come into gardens in rural areas. The sexes are the same. They have a chocolate-coloured cap, a white collar and a black mark on the cheek, and altogether have a cleaner, neater look than the house sparrows. They like grain, and are more likely to be seen on the ground than on the table.

There is a bird called a hedge sparrow, but it is not really a sparrow (see 'Dunnock' below).

Finches

There are four kinds of medium-sized finch that are very likely to turn up in gardens: the greenfinch, the goldfinch, the chaffinch and the bullfinch. All these finches are about sparrow-size, with fairly broad bills for attacking seeds. They get the 'finch' part of their name from the commmonest member of the family, the chaffinch, which has a loud 'pink, pink' or 'fink, fink' call. The chaffinch is actually called the *vink* in Holland.

The greenfinch is the finch most likely to come in large numbers to your garden. They flock together in winter to hunt for food, so if they find your peanuts there will be quite a crowd of them. They come in with a looping flight and a rattling twitter. The males are a lovely apple-green colour with noticeable golden-yellow patches on the wings; the females are the same, but a bit duller.

I mentioned earlier that you may find greenfinches strung all the way down a long feeder, one at every porthole, and on bird tables they arrive in a mob and are very aggressive. In summer you may also get a number of them down in the garden together, because they often nest in little groups near each other. They are helped greatly by mealworms or other insect food when they are bringing up their young.

Goldfinches are more delicate birds than greenfinches. They fly in as if they were feathers carried on the wind, with a light twitter that is like little bells also trembling in the wind. They are exceptionally beautiful birds, with a red, white and black head, like a tiny national flag, and gold wing bars. They are more nimble and acrobatic than the greenfinches, because like the tits they naturally swing under twigs to feed – mostly in alder and birch trees, where in autumn and winter they gather in flocks to eat the seeds. In summer, you may find you have one singing a tinkling song high in a treetop right into August, when most birds have stopped singing. We shall see later how they can also be attracted to a garden by thistle seeds growing there.

Chaffinches are the commonest finches in Britain, but not usually the commonest finch in any one garden. In fact, a single pair may patrol your garden all the year round. Chaffinches do also flock in winter, but many of these are winter immigrants from the continent, and are more likely to stay feeding in ploughed fields by a woodland edge. The males are pretty, pink-breasted birds, the females are brown, but both sexes have a distinctive double white wing-bar, and an unmistakable soft 'chup' call when they fly up. They feed happily on the ground and sometimes on the table, but they are not very acrobatic.

Bullfinches are shy visitors to bird tables, but are quite often seen there. Usually there will only be one pair around. The males have a rosier red breast than the chaffinches, while the females are brown beneath. They both have prominent black caps and a very noticeable white rump or lower back when they fly away. They mostly eat seeds, and have strong beaks to crack them, but they can also ravage the buds of fruit trees in the spring, and they feed their young on worms and caterpillars.

There are also two smaller finches that may visit gardens. Siskins are green finches that are noticeably smaller than greenfinches – in fact they are not much bigger than blue tits. In summer they are mainly found in conifer forests in the northern parts of Great Britain, but they spread throughout the country in winter. They feed in alders and birches along-side goldfinches, and in recent years have started coming regularly to gardens for the peanuts – especially, as noted, in red containers. A cloud of them whirling through the sky seem to be dropping a strange, whispering music from heaven.

Redpolls (sometimes called 'lesser redpolls') are another species of finch that sways upside down in alders and birches, and also occasion-ally on garden feeders. They are the size of siskins but are light brown birds with a bright red forehead and a black bib. They have a very harsh twitter as they fly.

Tits
These are the colourful acrobats of the garden. We get used to them, but if you stop to think about it, blue tits and great tits, with their blue, green, yellow and black plumage, are among the most beautiful birds in the world. We are lucky that that they are so common, with their numbers staying steady or even increasing.

Great tits are the biggest and have a cap and bib like a house sparrow, as well as a black line down their stomachs, which are a bright sulphur-yellow. Above, they are green and bluey-grey. They are very active and vigorous; when they land, they always look left and right.

They have sharp beaks, not so stout as a sparrow's or a finch's, but not as fine as a warbler's. They will eat most of the food you put out, but are particularly enthusiastic about peanuts, and are master swingers on the wire mesh.

On the bird table, if several of them come down, you will find there is a kind of 'pecking order' among them, with the weaker birds submitting to the dominant 'chiefs' and letting them take what they want first. The dominant great tits are the ones with the boldest black lines down their stomachs. In fact they all benefit from this way of life that has evolved among them. It means that they all spend less time quarrelling and more time feeding, and on a bird table there will probably be enough food at most times for the submissive birds to get a share.

Blue tits are smaller and bluer, but with an equally bright yellow breast. They have a distinctive black line that goes through each eye and curls down round their white cheeks. They lift their blue head feathers when they are excited. They are even more acrobatic than the great tits, since in natural conditions they spend most of their life upside down in trees, looking for moth eggs or caterpillars. In gardens, they are attracted to the same food as the great tits, and particularly like the hanging blocks of fat.

Long-tailed tits look quite different. They are black and white birds, with rose-tinted shoulders. Their long tails make them look like flying teaspoons. As has been mentioned, they have only started coming to feed in gardens in recent years, but the practice is steadily becoming more common. They are most likely to be seen on the feeders, where they hang without any difficulty.

Two other tits that are mainly woodland birds also come into gardens. Coal tits are the smallest tits, just under a blue tit in size, generally greyish in appearance, with a black cap and bib and a very distinctive white patch on the back of the neck. They are rollicking acrobats, and if you get one in your garden it will probably be having a go at the peanuts. They nest mainly in conifer trees, and spend a lot of time in them.

Marsh tits never move far from home and will only come to gardens near their natural haunts, which are dampish woodlands. They are like coal tits, but slightly bigger and without the white patch on the back of the head. They have become much rarer in recent years.

Thrushes

Two of the most regular garden visitors, the blackbird and the robin, belong to this family. You will also probably see song thrushes and mistle thrushes in the garden. Any of these four birds may be found trying to catch earthworms on the lawn. In wet weather, it is easier for them as the ground is soft and worms come nearer to the surface. They will stand with their heads cocked, listening for the sound of movement below the earth's surface, and if they hear a worm they will plunge their beaks in and try to pull it out. But when the ground is hard — whether because it is frozen in winter, or baked in summer — the supply of earthworms dries up.

They also eat slugs, and the song thrush will sometimes find a snail, take it to a convenient stone, and crack the snail shell open. You may find a heap of shells round a stone.

The robins are perhaps the most loved of the bird visitors. They are very trusting with human beings, sometimes crossing the doorstep of the kitchen and looking inside, or waiting on a fence while someone digs a vegetable patch, then hopping close to pick up a worm. They will also watch other creatures at work — for instance, when a mole is

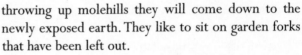

throwing up molehills they will come down to the newly exposed earth. They like to sit on garden forks that have been left out.

They are quite unmistakeable with their red breasts and olive-brown backs. The males and females are alike, but the young birds, when they first come out of the nest, have spotted brown breasts, which only turn red when they moult and grow new feathers in the autumn.

Unlike most birds, robins defend a territory both in the summer and the winter. The females are particularly unusual, for they hold their own territory in winter, and, like the males, sing to announce to other robins that they are the owner of it. 'So keep out!' they are saying. Very few female birds in other species sing a song like this.

In spring, the female robin joins a male and gives up her own territory. A neighbouring male and female quite often form a pair and amalgamate their holdings.

That is why in winter, you are likely to have only one regular robin in the garden. Others that come in will usually be chased away. If, from February onwards, you notice two of them near each other, and not fighting, they will probably be a mated pair that intend to nest some-where in the garden.

Although they are bold birds, they are very alert and quick to take alarm. They will come to bird tables, where, as has been said, they are especially fond of mealworms, but they will rarely stay there to eat. They prefer to carry some morsel off. In nature, they mostly feed on the ground, flitting down for an insect or spider they have seen, then flying up again.

Blackbirds are among the commonest garden visitors. The glossy black birds with yellow beaks are the males; the females are dark brown, with a slightly streaky breast. The males hold a territory in the spring and summer, and announce the fact with one of the most beautiful of bird songs – a lazy, mellow fluting that is the voice of the summer in town and country alike. But even in summer, several black-birds may come down together where food has been put out.

In winter, the native British population of blackbirds is joined by many visitors from as far away as Russia. When the ground is frozen or covered with snow, they will throng in places where food is made available for them. They quickly associate food with human beings in such places, whether parks or gardens, and at the sight of a person approaching will cluck plaintively. They quarrel a lot, and sometimes seem to lose by it, with a pigeon snapping up a piece of bread as two blackbirds fight over it. Like the robins, they are also quick to flee if they are frightened, but they will soon come back again.

They are relatively large birds, and need a lot of food to sustain them through a winter's day, so it is particularly desirable to help them in freezing weather. They will generally take food more readily on the ground, though at any time one may arrive on the bird table, lifting its long tail up in the air for a moment as it lands.

Song thrushes are much shyer than blackbirds. They tend to lurk under bushes and hedges and only come out on the lawn when they are sure that the coast is clear. They are a little smaller than blackbirds, and have brown upper parts and a boldly spotted or streaked breast. The spots seem to run down the breast in vertical lines. Though they are shy, they have a bold and upright demeanour, and can hop or run very fast. I like to see one sprinting across a lawn.

Oddly enough, though they are shy on the ground, the males sing one of the loudest – and finest – bird songs in Britain. It can be heard coming from the treetops from November or December right through to July, and there is no difficulty in seeing the bird up there, especially if the sun is shining on him. He often repeats a double or triple note several times before going on to another phrase – as the Victorian poet, Robert Browning wrote,

> That's the wise thrush;
> he sings each song twice over,
> Lest you should think he never could recapture
> The first fine careless rapture!

Song thrushes too may appear briefly on bird tables when all is quiet, but will benefit most from food – especially fruit – put down on the ground near cover.

The other fairly common thrush of the British countryside is the much larger mistle, or missel, thrush, which is almost as big as a small pigeon. It gets its name from its liking for mistletoe berries. It has larger spots on its breast than the song thrush, and the spots seem to run more horizontally. It has a loud churring call, and it shows a flash of silver under its wings when it flies.

It divides its time between the high treetops and the ground, but prefers to feed on wide stretches of grass, such as playing fields, rather than in gardens. Nevertheless, a large lawn may attract it, and it may be tempted to see what is available on a bird table.

Starlings

Starlings are unmistakable characters without any close relatives among the other garden birds. They look black at a glance, but in fact they are covered with fine, pale spots, and their bodies gleam with green and purple glosses when the light strikes them from the right angle. In spring, their beaks turn bright yellow and they might at a glance be mistaken for a male blackbird, but their short tails and their busy, bustling manner are quite different. They fly high and in the air they look star-shaped.

They are very bold and also very sociable. One minute you may have a whole crowd outside the window, next minute they have all flown off together. They often nest under the eaves of a house or behind a water pipe, and a male starling will sometimes sing its whirring, clicking song on a chimney-pot near its nest, and wave its wings when other starlings fly past to tell them to keep away. But their nests are often quite close together, and they feed together in flocks throughout the year.

They have strong sharp beaks, and will go anywhere and eat practically anything, but they are not acrobats. However, in late summer you may see flocks of them over the garden chasing flying ants in the sky.

Dunnocks

This is another species without any common relative in Britain. It has long been called the 'hedge sparrow' because, as has been remarked, it is not unlike a female house sparrow, but that misleading name has now generally given way to the older name of 'dunnock'. It is also sometimes called a 'hedge accentor'. In spring, the males sing a wispy thin little song in a bush ten or twelve feet from the ground – you often find them singing in flowering yellow laburnums, which are about the right height for them. Although the male's song sounds weak, nevertheless he often has two or even more mates. The dunnock is a shy, insect-eating bird that feeds on the ground and does not like going far from shelter. But like most of the shyer birds, it will sometimes come to a bird table.

Other species

Warblers are a large family of small, graceful insect-eating birds, many of them with fine songs. Nearly all the species found in Britain come here just for the summer, and more will be said about them when we come to the question of providing nesting habitats for birds.

However, a few blackcaps and chiffchaffs are found here in the winter months, probably birds that bred in Germany and got no further south than Britain on their autumn migration. Wintering blackcaps have taken to appearing at bird tables in recent years. The males are small grey birds with black caps, superficially similar to marsh tits. But a close look easily distinguishes them. The marsh tits have large black caps and bibs, whereas the blackcap only has a little skull-cap. (The female blackcap is even easier with its orange-brown cap.) Also, the blackcap is a delicate, slender bird that slips nervously onto the table, while the marsh tit is sturdy and confident. Chiffchaffs, which are small olive-green birds, with a shy, quick-moving demeanour similar to the blackcap's, may also sometimes arrive on the table in winter.

The smallest British bird, the goldcrest, is sometimes regarded as one of the warbler family. In winter, goldcrests travel around the countryside with flocks of tits. They are almost exclusively insect-eaters, hanging upside down among pine needles, but they can be tempted by grated cheese in hard weather. They are not hard to identify with their tiny size, their restless movements, their greenish bodies, and the brilliant splash of gold along the crown of their heads.

There are three tree-climbing birds that may like the food you put out. The largest is the great spotted woodpecker – a magnificent bird to see outside the window. It has bold black and white markings, and what looks like a big splash of bright red blood under its tail. The male also has a red forehead. It will hang on the feeders, and on the table will probably frighten all the other birds away.

The little blue-backed nuthatch is one of the most agile bird climbers. It can walk on a tree-trunk in any direction, and feeds largely on nuts, which it wedges in a crack in the bark and splits open with the aid of its strong neck muscles and powerful beak. But it is quite happy to have an easy life eating your peanuts.

The treecreeper – which is brown like tree-bark above, silvery white below – goes slowly up the tree-trunks probing for insects with its tiny, curved bill, and may flit down to the bird table. An alternative way of attracting, and helping, nuthatches and treecreepers is to smear fat on the tree-trunks in your garden.

Finally, what about sparrowhawks? They will come to the garden not to eat the food you provide, but to eat the birds for which you are providing it. Normally they flit along the hedges, trying to catch small birds by surprise as they swing suddenly across to the other side. So for them, a little knot of birds on a bird table is a juicy target if they can rush up to it without warning. They pick up a great tit in their claws and whirl away with it.

Are they to be regarded as your enemies? It could be said that you are simply their benefactor, too. Most birds eat living things, and sparrowhawks do the same – it just happens that what evolution has led them to eat is other birds. They are no more cruel than a robin with a worm.

You may prefer to fend them off with a roof over your bird table, though that is by no means certain protection for the birds beneath. For my own part, I prefer to regard them simply as part of nature, and let them live as they will. What is more, they are a very dramatic sight as they swoop down, brake with a rushing sound in their wings, and rocket away again, sometimes with a victim in their talons, but more often thwarted again.

Last thoughts on feeding

Apart from the pleasure you get from seeing the birds, is there any other reason for feeding them? Birds have fended for themselves since long before the days of mankind, and there are still plenty of them around, so do they need the food that people put out for them?

If a population of birds is to remain stable, for each pair that is alive in a given summer, there only needs to be one pair still alive, and in a condition to breed, the following summer. So if both parents of a brood of young birds are still alive and can still breed the following year, it will not have been necessary, from the population point of view, for any of their offspring to have survived at all. Similarly, if both the parents die, they will only need to have produced two surviving young birds.

However, most pairs of blackbirds, to take an example, try to rear at least two broods a year of four or five birds each. If they all survived, there would be about five times as many blackbirds around the following year. Yet, as our eyes tell us, and scientific studies have shown, there is very rarely much of an increase in the population from year to year.

That means that most of the summer population of adults and young regularly dies before the winter is over, probably because there is simply not enough food to support them in the winter months. From year to year, unless circumstances change, only about two birds do in fact appear to survive from each family every year, and so the population stays roughly the same.

If fewer than two birds survive from each family of parents and young, then the population of that species will suffer a setback. That may happen after a particularly hard winter, especially to small birds such as wrens and long-tailed tits, among whom there may be serious starvation.

Yet even these populations quickly recover if the next few winters are milder. If there are fewer families around to breed after a hard winter, clearly more birds from each family are going to find enough food to get through the next winter, providing it is mild – and with long-tailed tits and wrens, which both lay large clutches of eggs, there is always a big pool of young birds available for survival, so to speak. So in this second summer after the hard winter there will be more birds breeding than there were in the previous year, even if not there are not so many as there were in the summer before the hard winter.

So it goes on; and in this way, the population climbs again from year to year, until it once more reaches the maximum that the land can support.

It might seem, therefore, that there is no particular point in giving supplementary food to birds in a hard winter. Enough will survive, it would seem, for the population to recover eventually from any losses due to shortage of food.

But that view is a very narrow one. In the first place, it ignores the simple humanitarian impulse not to let birds suffer and starve, if we can do anything about it. A great many birds will die every winter, no matter what we do – but why not help as many as we can? Apart from the pleasure of having them around, this is probably the main reason that people are impelled to feed the birds.

Next, even if we are only thinking of our desire to have birds round the house and garden because we like seeing and hearing them, we might want to try to keep the local population up in a hard winter as much as we can – and indeed do our bit, at the same time, for the national population.

We may not be content simply with the thought that the numbers will recover in due course. We do not want them to fall, as far as we can help it, in the first place. Birds themselves may not be aware of it when their numbers have gone down, but we are.

Most important, though, is that little phrase I used just now, 'unless circumstances change'. In the twenty-first century, circumstances are changing for birds. Above all, new agricultural methods, especially the vastly increased use of herbicides and pesticides, have sharply reduced the quantity of weed seeds and insects available to birds in the countryside. And the numbers of many birds have declined significantly, especially in farmland, with this drop in food supplies.

There seems every reason to believe that garden bird feeding can help to make up for those losses with certain species. Song thrushes have experienced a major decline in their numbers in farmland. Even in gardens, they may be suffering from eating slugs that have been poisoned with chemicals. There are less than half as many of them in Britain as there were 25 years ago. They certainly need help – even if they are not the easiest birds to help – and everything that garden owners do for them must be useful, as long as it is kept up. Just recently, at last, their numbers seem to have picked up again slightly.

Blackbirds and starlings have also gone down substantially in abundance over the last 25 years, and these birds can easily be helped in gardens. We have already seen that this is the case with house sparrows. It may make a difference. Redpolls have suffered heavy losses over a very short period and it is particularly desirable to attract them to gardens and feed them.

Even the birds whose populations are not obviously under threat may be maintaining their position partly due to human support with food. Greenfinches used to roam the countryside looking for weed seeds, and the way they now flock into gardens may be a reflection of their difficulty in finding this wild food. So many blue tits and great tits feed in gardens that it is hard not to believe that this has some influence on their reasonably healthy numbers. The enormous robin population of Britain is largely in gardens and must be to some degree dependent on man.

Nuthatches and blackcaps have, I am glad to say, doubled in number in Britain in recent years – but I do not think that can be attributed to garden feeding. In fact the increase in numbers might be the reason that they come into gardens more – a delightful turn of events.

One question that is often asked is whether birds should be fed in the summer. Certainly they should be fed until late in the spring if you wish to help them. I have spoken of the heavy winter mortality suffered by birds, and much of this takes place as late as March. By that time most of the berries and seeds, and the easily accessible insects and insect eggs on the trees, have run out, and it is a month when birds find it particularly hard to get sufficient food, even if the weather is good. So feeding should certainly go on until the new insects and seeds are becoming plentiful.

As for the summer, feeding during the breeding period used to be discouraged. It was thought that the kind of food that is mostly put out in gardens is not ideal nourishment for young birds in the nest – but that their parents might take the easy way and feed it to them. That does not seem to happen very much. The parents are more discriminating than was thought.

In fact, if the parents come to bird tables and feeders in the summer it is probably to get food for themselves. And that can increase their chances of bringing up their young successfully. They must eat too – and they have to work very hard when feeding their brood. If good food is readily available for them, it makes that short but intense period in their lives much easier.

This is especially important if they have been encouraged to nest in the garden by the provision of nest boxes. The garden may be further away from good food supplies both for themselves and their young than a natural home would be. That means they have to travel further and use up more energy to find it. If you give them a home, give them food as well, or you may find dead babies in the boxes. As for the provision of the homes, we shall turn to that in the next chapter.

CHAPTER FOUR

Making a Home For The Birds

Feeding birds in winter will attract many visitors to your garden, and some of them will continue to come in the spring and summer if you go on putting food out. But you can go further and encourage them to build their nests and bring up their broods in the garden too.

Putting up nest boxes, or bird boxes as they are sometimes called, is nowadays the principal way of doing this. The two species that most readily accept man-made nest boxes as a home for their family are the great tit and the blue tit.

In nature, they both nest in holes in trees or other such crevices. Among other natural nesting sites, great tits have also been recorded as using holes burrowed out in banks by kingfishers and sand martins, and hollows in the bottom of the old nests of other birds, including jays and rooks. They often use man-made objects such as flower pots, outdoor letter boxes and empty pipes, and there is a record of a pair building an enormous nest right across the floor of an old beehive. It is not surprising that they have welcomed the arrival of nest boxes on the scene, and Christopher Perrins, the author of a book on *British Tits*, has gone so far as to say that 'it is relatively easy to induce all the pairs of great tits in given area to accept nesting boxes'.

Blue tits will also make use of a great variety of natural and man-made sites, including old cans and street lamps. They used to like the old gas lamps on the roadside, where the gas pipe came out of the pillar into the lantern, leaving quite a deep, broad space all round it inside the pillar. They are now almost as keen on nest boxes as the great tits, though being smaller they manage more easily to find natural holes and cracks to use.

Other regular users of garden nest boxes are starlings – who will sometimes turn tits out of a box if the hole is large enough for them to get into it – and house sparrows, robins, pied wagtails and spotted flycatchers. You might even get coal tits or nuthatches. Most of them need somewhat different kinds of box, and that is what we shall consider next.

How to build or choose a nest box

Tit boxes are the nest boxes chosen by most people. The design is essentially the same for both blue tits and great tits. The main difference is that great tits need a slightly bigger hole.

It is quite easy to make a simple wooden nest box oneself – and on the whole, a simple box is all that the titmice want.

You need six pieces of wood cut to the right shape and size – a back

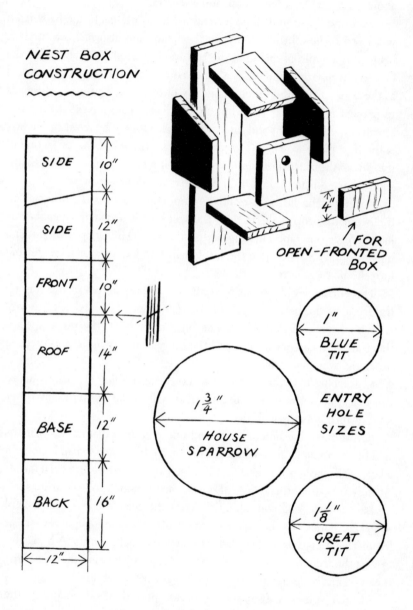

NEST BOX
CONSTRUCTION

SIDE	10"
SIDE	12"
FRONT	10"
ROOF	14"
BASE	12"
BACK	16"

12"

4"

FOR
OPEN-FRONTED
BOX

1"
BLUE
TIT

$1\frac{3}{4}$"
HOUSE
SPARROW

ENTRY
HOLE
SIZES

$1\frac{1}{8}$"
GREAT
TIT

and a front, two sides, a bottom and a lid. The finished box should be about a foot wide, a foot deep, and a foot tall.

Since the lid should slope downward from the back, the back itself will need to be a little taller than the front, and also needs a further, projecting couple of inches at the top and bottom by which to nail the box to a tree trunk. The sides also, of course, need to slope downward at the top, so that the lid closes neatly onto them. The lid itself needs to project a little over the front so that water running off it does not stream down the front and into the entrance hole. The front of the box is the best place in which to make the hole, though it can be in one of the sides. About the bottom there is nothing to be said – except that it should have a little hole in it in case any rain does get in.

Fastening the lid on carefully is important. It must be attached to the projecting top at the back of the box by a broad strip of rubber or leather or stout tape running across the box. This strip will act as a hinge, folding as you open the lid. It will also keep water from getting into the box at the rear of the lid.

The entrance hole needs to be about three-quarters of the way up the front of the box. The size of the hole depends on what birds you want to keep out of the box. The bigger the hole, the more species there are that can get into it, and the biggest ones will usually succeed in taking over the box.

So for blue tits you want a small hole that nothing else can squeeze through – about an inch in diameter. It will be surprising if any other kind of bird gets through that.

If you make the hole an inch and one-eighth in diameter, great tits will be the most likely tenants. A blue tit could of course live happily in a box with a hole of this size, but if it tries to, a great tit may turn it out. At the same time, this hole will not be large enough to let starlings in.

Lastly, you need something to keep the lid closed. A resourceful squirrel might easily be able to open it otherwise, and squirrels are as happy to eat eggs or young birds as they are to eat peanuts. A hook and eye on the front are probably the best means of fastening the lid so that it can be easily be opened and closed again when required.

Also, if you have squirrels or great spotted woodpeckers in the garden, a metal panel around the hole will prevent them from gnawing or pecking at the wood around the hole to enlarge it and get at the occupants. You can buy these plates ready-made for different-sized holes. You can also buy a short length of pipe to fit round the hole to make it harder for intruders to get a beak or paw in.

The box should be coated with creosote or some other waterproof preserver when it is finished. But do not coat the inside of the box.

You can easily buy a simple box of the kind I have been describing, and they are not very expensive. But make sure it has all the features I have mentioned. Above all, it must be waterproof and safe for its inhabitants.

You can also buy other, more elaborate boxes. There are rustic boxes just as there are rustic bird tables, but it is best to be wary of them. A hollowed-out birch log looks pretty, but it may quickly rot. (However, you could make a rough-and-ready bird box yourself from a hollowed-out log of some sound wood.)

There are variations on the standard nest box – a gabled roof, for example, sloping to left and right, or sides themselves that slope from top to bottom so that the box looks like a tent, or a box with an entrance at the front.

It is also possible now to buy nest boxes made of 'woodcrete', a substance made of wood and cement. These are more expensive, but are strong and enduring, and keep out the wind and rain without any problem. They are also warmer for the birds, and keep a more constant temperature inside.

For other species than the titmice, a different style of nest box will be more successful. House sparrows need a larger hole – about an inch and three-quarters in diameter – and since they are sociable nesters, you can get a long, terrace-shaped box with a hole on each side as well as one at the front, in which you may find up to three of their raggedy nests in a row. Of course a pair of sparrows will also use a simple nest box if the hole is large enough.

Not many people want to provide a nest box for starlings, who may be nesting under the roof of the house or behind a water pipe in any case. But they may come to a box with a large entrance-hole

The other main design of nest box is the open-fronted box. Birds that like nesting in hollows, rather than in holes in trees, will generally be more attracted by these. They are the same as the tit box except for having only a low wall at the front and a large space above it for the birds to enter by. They make their nest behind the wall in the depths of the box, and the bird sitting on its eggs can look out over the wall and see what it is happening in the world outside. These boxes are most suitable for robins, pied wagtails and spotted flycatchers. We shall come to boxes for larger birds, such as kestrels and owls, when we turn to the possibilities in more extensive gardens.

Where to put your box – or boxes

Tit boxes can be nailed up anywhere in the garden that is easy of access for the birds and safe from predators.

Some of the points we considered when discussing where to put a bird table are also relevant here. The box should be high enough for cats not to be able to jump up to it easily. It should be at least five feet above the ground, and can be anything up to fifteen feet up. As far as possible, too, it should be hard for cats and squirrels to approach from other directions, though that is often asking too much – which is why it needs to be a strongly protected little fortress in the way we have described.

One small point is that it is not desirable to have a perch built into the box by the entrance hole. That gives a predatory bird something to sit on, while the nesting birds themselves will actually prefer to fly straight into the hole without pausing. They are good shots, skilful at doing that.

Again as with a bird table, it is better if there is a bush or tree fairly near the box so that the birds can look about them and be sure that the coast is clear before they shoot across into the box. But the box should not be so close to the branches that animals can easily spring on to it from them.

The direction in which the box faces is a further point to consider. It is better if does not face south into the sun at its hottest, and also if it does not face between south-west and north-west into the often rainy winds from that quarter.

You can also hang a nest box from a branch by a rope or chain. Birds seem to feel particularly safe in boxes like that, even though they may sway in the wind.

The open-fronted boxes need to be sited differently to attract the kinds of birds that they are intended for. Robins are your most likely guests and are as common in town gardens as in country gardens. In nature, robins nest in holes in hedge-banks, behind loose bark on a tree and in many similar hollows. I once found a robin's nest in a hole in the ground. I glanced down among some young bracken and saw the beady eyes of the sitting bird looking up at me from the earth. They are also famous for nesting in such places as old kettles and the glove compartments of abandoned cars, or even in corners of cars or vans that are still being used.

So it is best to put a box for robins on an ivy-covered wall, or on the ledge of a shed – either outdoors or indoors (providing that a window or door is kept open) – making sure that it is firmly attached.

Spotted flycatchers often nest in gardens in the wisteria on the wall of a house. They use a horizontal branch up against the wall, half-hidden by leaves and flowers. You can put your nest-box in just such a place, again attaching it firmly – and a spotted flycatcher that may not hitherto have found just what it wanted in your wisteria may now be induced to stay. Similar sites against a wall with a little shelter – climbing roses, for example – may also be acceptable. It ought to be ten or twelve feet up.

Pied wagtails are great searchers-out of cracks and crevices in all sorts of places – in walls, in stacks of firewood, in thatched roofs – and sometimes they will use an old song thrush's or blackbird's nest. They run about on the roofs of houses, singing and looking for insects and spiders, but they are not primarily garden birds, and are most likely to nest in a large garden with a lawn – where they also like running about, wagging their long tails.

If you want to try to persuade a pair to nest, find some sheltered hollow, not too near the house, which as it stands offers no good surface to build on, and put your box there. But you might end up with anything from a blackbird to a wren nesting in it!

There is no reason why you should not have a number of nest boxes in the garden, but it is best not to have too many. Tit boxes will only be occupied at some distance from each other, since each pair likes a bit of territory round their nest. House sparrows, as has been said, are less troubled by neighbours. As to robins, spotted flycatchers or pied wag-tails, you are not likely to have more than one nest in the garden of any of these species.

Put the boxes some distance from the bird table, too. Your nest box tenants will almost certainly be glad to use the bird table, but they will be distracted at the nest if there is too much noisy coming and going of other birds just by their door.

It is best to put your boxes up in the autumn. That is no guarantee that they will attract birds to nest in them in the spring, but the longer they are there, the more familar they will become to the birds in the garden, and that will increase your chances. When, early in the year, birds start to choose the area in which they will try to hold a spring and summer territory, they look out for potential nesting sites among other things and will certainly take your boxes into consideration.

Boxes put up in the autumn will also probably be used for night-time roosting by birds during the winter. If they are, it is best to give them a spring-clean as the days begin to draw out.

What you may see the nesting birds doing

If blue tits and great tits make their territory in or around your garden, you will be able to watch the different phases of the breeding cycle. Both species will be singing from early in the year. The great tit has a loud, unmistakable song – a repeated 'teacher, teacher, teacher' from up in a tree. It has been aptly compared to someone steadily pumping up a bicycle tyre with a squeaky pump. The great tit also has a loud 'chink chink' call and other notes. The blue tit has a quieter song, con-sisting of a few thin notes followed by a rapid trill. Like the great tit, it will repeat its song again and again, and it also has a number of other wispy spring calls.

It is the males who sing the songs. It is their way, as with other birds, of announcing that they are in possession of a territory, and also of attracting a mate if they need to.

Blue tits

Many pairs of blue tits seem to stay together thoughout the winter, so the male has no need to lure a female in the spring. But some birds lose their mate, while birds born the previous year have to find their first mate and, if they are males, carve out their first territory, and among these there is a good deal of chasing about in the trees in February and March before they all settle down.

Early in the year the blue tits will also start inspecting nest sites, and you may see them popping in and out of your box or boxes to see what they have to offer. The male sometimes leads the female to the box and to other possible nesting sites for her to consider them.

It will be the middle of April, though, before they start to think seriously about nesting. Then, if they choose your box, the female may spend the night in it for a few weeks before she starts to build their nest. After that, you will see her taking in moss and twigs and strips of bark to make a firm foundation for the nest and then carrying in feathers to make a soft bed for the eggs and for herself. Some females start bringing twigs laid across their beak and cannot get through the entrance hole with them. They soon learn to bring them length-wise and pull them in behind them. The male often accompanies the female while she is building and goes into the hole to look around, but he does not usually help her.

You may also see courtship displays, such as a curious moth-like flight round the female by the male, and may even see the actual mating of the pair. But this is usually a very rapid action, lasting only a few seconds. The female crouches, the male settles on her back and in a moment inserts his sperm; then they fly apart.

The female will lay between seven and fourteen eggs in the nest, one a day, usually in the morning, and will cover them with the feathers until she is ready to begin incubating them. She will start sitting on them when the clutch is complete, or just before – she may lay another egg after she has begun to incubate.

She keeps them warm with her body for about a fortnight. She has a patch of bare skin on her stomach, called a brood patch, that is dense with blood-vesssels. It fits over the eggs and keeps them close to blood temperature. The male does not help her with the incubation of the eggs, but you may see him going in sometimes to feed her with small caterpillars. She will come off the nest from time to time while she is sitting, but she will not stay away from her eggs for long.

Now we meet the question of whether you should look into the box. Many garden owners feel that they would like to have a glimpse of the eggs and, later, the young birds. That should do no harm, provided one is careful and discreet. While the clutch is being completed, and the birds are away from the nest, is a good time to have a look – going up a ladder, and briefly opening the lid and peering in. Touching the eggs or taking them out is not such a good idea, since such tiny, fragile things are easily broken. But they are to my mind beautiful objects, with their pearly-white shells lightly speckled with reddish-brown. After a peep like this, don't forget to close the lid firmly and move the ladder away again.

Once the female is sitting, it is best to look only when she is off the nest. If you startle her off the nest by opening the lid, especially in the first days after she has begun to sit, she may desert the nest. So it is desirable to watch and wait for her to come out of the hole before you attempt to see the eggs.

Incidentally, the female is almost identical to the male, except for being a little duller. But by watching the pair together, you may get to know which is which and to recognise them from slight individual differences.

When the eggs hatch, the male will start bringing food for the young. The female will stay mainly on the nest for the first few days after hatching, keeping the tiny nestlings warm, especially in a cold spell. (This is where the 'woodcrete' boxes help with their even temperature.) After that she will join the male in collecting food.

The parents will have a very busy time now. The young will probably hatch in the first half of May, when the oak trees are covered with the caterpillars of various moths. Evolution has programmed the birds' inner timing so that they have this abundance of food just when it is needed. But you may find that you can still help them with peanuts and seed and mealworms.

Now you will see the parents going in and out of the box all day. It is all right to look in at their family occasionally – especially when the parents are not about. At first you will find naked-looking little birds with just a little greyish-white down on them, and they will probably lift their beaks hoping you are their parents coming with food. The beaks are reddish inside with a yellow rim.

Over the next two or three weeks they will grow and change rapidly, until they are chubby little creatures almost as big as their parents and with a full coat of feathers. The main difference now between them and their parents is that they have yellow, not white cheeks. It is best not to look at them once they have got most of their feathers, or you might frighten them out of the nest before they are ready. This is particularly important when they are on the point of flying.

One day, probably at the end of May or early in June, they will be ready to fly. If your timing is lucky, you may see some ten or a dozen little yellow-cheeked birds come streaming out of the box. When one leaves, they all leave.

Their parents will go on feeding them for a while, and if they stay around the garden you may hear one of the characteristic sounds of June, the thin 'see-see-see' calls of the fledglings insistently begging for food in the depths of the bushes. But the young birds will be soon be flying well and looking after themselves, and eventually the family will wander off.

The parents will not normally breed again that year. Late broods are generally the result of the parents losing their first brood. If you open the box now, you may find in it the body of a small nestling who was never strong enough to compete with his brothers and sisters, or an unhatched egg. (These are about the only wild birds' eggs you are allowed by law to take.) It is time to take the box down and clean it, and nail it up again for winter roosting.

Great tits

The breeding cycle of the great tit is broadly similar to that of its smaller relative, though nest-building usually begins a little later, towards the end of April. If you find you have a nest in the box but have not seen the birds at work building it, you can generally distinguish between a great tit's and a blue tit's by the lining material. Unlike the blue tits, the great tits do not use many feathers, but prefer to make the soft bed out of hair or fur, which they are clever at finding. They like horsehair that has got entangled on a barbed wire fence. The cup is also bigger than the one the blue tits make, because the eggs will be bigger and so will the bird sitting on them.

Events in the nest-box will be much the same as they are with blue tits. The reddish blotches on the eggs are sometimes larger and more scattered. The male great tit, like the male blue tit, will feed his mate on caterpillars, and help to feed the young. The beaks of the latter are orange inside, and the edges pale yellow – you can see that when they are lifted up at you like small funnels when you look in. When they leave the nest, the fledglings are browner and greyer than their colourful parents, but they have the same yellow cheeks as the young blue tits, and they call in the bushes in June in just the same way. You can see how closely the two species are related.

House sparrows

These are wilder creatures than the tits. In the spring, mobs of male sparrows, all chirping excitedly, will chase a female sparrow into a bush or hedge, apparently trying to peck at her sexual organs. Altogether, house sparrows are more sexually active than many other birds. They pair up in a fairly normal way, but the couple mate very frequently and conspicuously – this is why in Alexander Pope's poem, *Epistle to Cobham*, the old roué 'envies every sparrow that he sees'. Sometimes a male has two mates. They also go on breeding throughout the spring and summer, often bringing up three broods of young in a year, and sometimes as many as five.

The male's song is little more than an energetic run of its usual chirping calls. He also has a loud double chirp in spring, which can go on and on from a roof top.

As we have seen, sparrows do not mind nesting close together. They find nesting places in holes under the eaves or in other parts of a building, and also in thick ivy and in dense, twiggy bushes. The nests in bushes are often quite neat, with a domed top, but the nests under any kind of roof are ragged affairs of straw, with other odd materials such as paper and string woven in, and a lining of hair and wool and feathers. A nest in a bird box will be like this, and in a 'sparrow terrace' there may be two or three of them.

Both sexes help to build the nest, but oddly enough the male does more of the work. You can see them flying about with straw in their beaks as early as January if the days are warm, or as late as in an Indian summer, but serious breeding goes on from about May till August.

The female house sparrow lays a small clutch – three to five eggs, all very blotchy, but varying in colour from one bird to another. The blotches may be brown, bluish-grey, greenish-grey or purple. The female does most of the incubating, but the male helps her feed the young. This is another case of the adults being mainly seed-eating birds, but giving insects to their offspring. They will make good use of a well-stocked bird table.

Looking into a lidded nest box that has been occupied by sparrows should follow the same rules as with the tits. If a sparrow builds in an open-fronted nest box, by approaching cautiously you should be able to see if the female is on the nest without disturbing her, and you can choose your moment to have a look at the eggs or young.

You might not like what you find. There can be sexual tragedies among these soap-opera sparrows. A male sparrow sometimes comes into the nest of a female who has another mate and kills all her babies. She will now want to start a new family and the murdering male hopes he will be able to lure away her away as his own partner this time.

Starlings

From early spring you may see a male starling looking into holes and singing on a branch or chimney pot close to one of them. It is the one that he and his mate will probably nest in and he wants to make sure no other pair will try to take it over. If he chooses a nest box, he will keep great tits and other small birds out.

It is he who starts the nest off, with a lot of dry stalks and leaves. He often does this even before he has a mate and the nest hole is one of the offerings he makes in order to get one. If you see two starlings going around together in the garden after a male appears to have taken up residence there, then he has probably found a female for himself. She will take over work on the nest from about the middle of April, lining it with feathers and moss and sheep wool if there is any in the neighbourhood.

However, do not be surprised to find a small flock of starlings still feeding on your lawn. They are sociable birds, even though they guard their nest hole jealously, and they continue to look for food together, often in quite big parties, throughout the summer. They also go back at evening to roost with other starlings until quite near breeding time.

The female lays about six very beautiful pale blue eggs. Sometimes you find one perfectly intact on a path – female starlings seem to be rather careless at times about where they lay. At other times they will deposit their eggs in another female's nest, and leave it to her to bring up their brood. If you find twelve eggs in your box, you will know what has happened.

Laying begins early in May and both parents take part in sitting on the eggs. Sometimes, when his mate is sitting, the male bird will continue to bring leaves or even flowers to the nest.

The young birds hatch out a fortnight, or a little less, after the start of incubation. Most starlings in a given area nest at about the same time, and once the young are out of the egg the sky around looks like an airport – full of starlings, both male and female, flying busily to and fro, finding food for their young and hurrying home with it! If you look in the box to see the small nestlings lifting their heads for food, you will find that the inside of their beaks is yellow.

They stay almost three weeks in the nest, and as they get bigger they become very noisy, greeting their harassed parents with a fierce-sounding churring note. Even when they leave the nest they go on calling for food, and the trees around are full of loud commotion. Soon they all come down on the grass to feed together, and you can pick out the young ones by their brown plumage and pale throats. They still go harassing their parents for a while, even chasing them through the sky.

Robins

We have seen how the male and female robin join up in the early spring – often around February 14, St Valentine's Day, the day when the birds are supposed to mate. The male's song seems to take on a particular beauty in the spring, though it still has its slightly sad quality. It is a rich, sweet outburst, followed every time by a wistful, falling phrase.

The robins start nesting earlier than the tits and starlings. In a warm spring, the female may be at work on her nest by the end of March or early April. If she chooses an open-fronted nest box she will fill it with dead leaves and moss and make a cup for the eggs out of hair and fine roots. Robins do not use feathers very much.

Male robins are among the most ardent practitioners of 'courtship feeding'. The female lowers her wings and shivers with excitement as the male comes up with a worm. As he passes it to her, she makes a strange, thin, tremulous note. No one knows quite the purpose of this ceremony, but it seems to help in binding the pair together emotionally. The food itself does not seem to be very important, since the male robin does not stuff his beak with food as he does when feeding the young, and in any case the female could probably pick up as much food herself in the time spent on the performance.

The female robin lays five or six eggs, white or bluish-white with reddish markings. Some individuals' eggs are only lightly spotted, some are a mass of speckles or blotches. The female alone sits on the eggs, but the male brings her food. At this stage, his worms and insects become definitely valuable, since they mean she does not have to leave the eggs to feed herself so often.

When the bird is sitting, one can often see the top of her head or her tail as one passes the nest, and one can become quite skilful at telling at a glance if she is 'on'. If the box is in ivy or creeper, it is best to interfere with it as little as possible. As with other nests, it should be looked at only when the bird is 'off'.

Also, one should be very careful not to disturb any leaves that hide or half-hide the nest. Magpies and jays are very curious and sharp-eyed, and may come down to investigate a shift of the foliage. If they find the nest, that will be the end of the eggs or chicks.

The eggs are incubated for about a fortnight and after about the same length of time, during which they are fed by both parents, the young are fully feathered and ready to fly. The spotty fledglings are looked after for some time afterwards, and from the depth of bushes comes exactly the same tremulous note as was heard in them five or six weeks earlier – for the young who are being fed cry out exactly as their mother did.

Robins can nest two or three times in the course of the summer, but they are not likely to nest in the same place more than once in a year. So after they have gone, clean out the nest box and put it back – and you may get something else.

Spotted flycatchers

Spotted flycatchers are late arrivals from Africa, not arriving till the end of April or early May. They are inconspicuous brown birds, until they fly out from a tree, snap up a passing insect and return to the perch they started from. They are also quiet birds on arrival, with a soft, squeaky song that is not often heard.

They will not start nesting till late May or even early June. The female does most of the building, weaving grass and small twigs together with spiders' webs, and lining the nest with feathers. (Where do all these feathers come from? it might be asked. I think that a lot of them are small white feathers that woodpigeons shed when they burst wildly out of thick bushes and trees.)

The female sits on the eggs. You can usually see her from below, looking up at her nest in the creeper, with her looking back at you with the eye on one side of her head. It is probably best not to climb up to look at her five mottled eggs, with all the disturbance to the foliage that will entail. You may be able to see into the nest from a window above it.

The male brings insects to the nest for the first few days after hatching, while the female broods the nestlings. Then they work together feeding the young. You may see some spectacular flycatching flights, with the bird twisting and turning as it pursues an insect.

It is after the young leave the nest – much more spotted than their parents – that the flycatchers become noisy. They feed their brood in the treetops for about three weeks, and they never stop giving alarm cries – a loud, quite unmistakable 'see-tic-tic, see-tic-tic' repeated again and again. They may have a second brood in a different nest, and repeat the whole performance.

Other birds

Pied wagtails may use an open-fronted nest box but, as has been said, they are not especially garden birds. They are resident birds, around all the winter, with the male warbling cheerfully on rooftops. Their black and white plumage, and their long tails, in ceaseless up-and-down motion, make them very attractive and welcome to most people. They have a deep, looping flight, calling 'chissick' loudly as they go.

The female, who is greyer on the back than her mate, builds the nest and he helps her with incubating and with feeding the young. When they are all out on the lawn together they make a spirited party, darting to and fro after flies and making little leaps in the air.

You may also get surprises in your nest box. It is always possible that a coal tit will use one of the blue tit boxes. While the female sits, the male will sing a speeded-up version of the great tit's 'teacher, teacher' song in a garden pine.

A pair of nuthatches may take over a box with a bigger entrance. In trees, they often use a deep gash in a branch or trunk and, to keep intruders out, plaster up most of the entrance with a dry mud wall, leaving only a little hole for themselves to go in and out. It is very interesting to see them doing this, using their beaks as tools, and they might do it on one of your boxes. If you have nuthatches nesting in your garden, they will certainly make use of your peanut feeders.

You may also be able to provide a home for that other small tree-climbing bird, the treecreeper, using a special box. They usually nest behind a loose piece of bark. The special treecreeper boxes are solid boxes nailed to a tree with a semi-circular hole right up against the trunk on one side, so that the birds can creep in from the trunk just as they would if they were going behind loose bark. The young, when they emerge, can climb as easily as their parents, and I once saw an adult treecreeper going straight up a tree trunk with a line of little young ones following behind it.

CHAPTER FIVE

The Lawn, The Flowers. The Trees

Most people want a garden for its grass and flowers and trees, its shadows and sunshine, its colours and its scents. Quite apart from setting up bird tables and nest boxes, what can you do to attract birds to a normal garden like that?

In fact, many of the plants you might want to have in the garden for their own sake are also very attractive to birds. First we shall consider such plants from the point of view of the food they might provide for birds with – and again we will start on the ground.

The grass

A lawn is a pleasure for humans and birds alike. Those birds that feed on it feel tolerably safe because, although they are exposed, they have a good view around and above them. It gives them time to spot and flee from a cat or a sparrowhawk.

There are often small insects among the blades of grass that birds will pick up, but the most interesting items for hungry birds are below the surface. Chief among these are earthworms which, as we have seen, come near to the surface when the soil is damp. They pull down dead leaves and other litter into their holes beneath the grass – that is their food. But a blackbird or song thrush cocking its head can hear them down below. Plunging its beak in, it often succeeds in pulling them out instead.

Other creatures live beneath the grass, many of them feeding on its roots. In summer, you may see a daddy-long-legs, or crane fly, settling on the grass to lay her little black eggs in the earth with her long ovipositor. The eggs hatch out into tough-skinned, greyish brown larvae, called leatherjackets, which are an important item of food for rooks on farmland, and also popular with starlings on lawns. Other insects out of sight among the grass roots are the caterpillars of various moths, including the large yellow underwing moth. The caterpillars are more often eaten by birds than the moths themselves. The moths, which may be common in the garden in late summer, hide their yellow hindwings under their brown front wings, and startle an inquisitive starling by suddenly flying up and flashing them.

If you want to make the lawn attractive to birds, it is probably best to let the grass cuttings and other litter lie on it. If you mow the lawn frequently, you will scatter the cuttings and they will not form unattractive mats. The cut grass and leaves will nourish the soil with the nitrogen, phosphorus and potassium in them – and the earthworms will help this process, both by making holes through which the dry grass will slip down into the soil and by actually dragging this vegetable matter down themselves. The earthworms will also contribute to the health of the soil beneath the lawn by breaking it up and aerating it.

So by leaving the litter, you will help the worms and they in turn will help the lawn. Meanwhile, the flourishing worm population will provide good feeding for the birds, who will come to look for them not only on rainy days but also when you have given the lawn a good watering. The birds will never eat so many earthworms that the number of them in the ground will be seriously affected.

The starlings, when they come down in a flock, may make quite a lot of deep holes in the lawn. They plunge their beaks into the ground and then cunningly open them to create the holes, so that they can poke around among the grass roots. You may find the holes unsightly. But the holes will help the lawn in the same way as the earthworms' holes do and will soon fill up and disappear.

Earthworms also live, of course, in the earth in flowerbeds and vegetable beds and birds will look for them there too. You can even boost the number of worms in your garden. Bird food specialists and organic gardening shops actually sell packs that contain a thousand earthworms or more for putting into your soil – specially recommended for the gardens of new houses where the soil may be poor.

There are also devices for putting large numbers of worms into your compost or your kitchen waste. They break up the compost or waste, aerating it and turning it into wormcasts, and the whole lot, worms and all, can from time to time be tipped into the garden.

So far we have talked only about animal life that is available for birds on or under the lawn. But the lawn may provide seeds for them too. To be realistic, not many people want dandelions on their lawn, spreading their rosettes of leaves across it, or even groundsel at the edge of the lawn, but those two flowers do draw goldfinches and greenfinches down to the grass. The birds come down for the seeds in spring and early summer when there are not yet many other new seeds to be had, and they can be a charming sight, picking out the umbrella-like seeds from the dandelion clocks or the groundsel's little white tufts and globules of seed.

Attractive flowers and bushes

What you plant in your garden may also make a difference to the number of birds you have feeding in it. We want flowers and bushes and trees for our own pleasure, but the insect life on them and the seeds and berries will interest the birds and bring them into the garden too.

Insects
A basic rule, if you want to attract birds, is not to use pesticides more than you can help. There may be plagues of aphids on the roses or the cabbages that you really have to do something about, but those little insects can help to feed many a young blue tit in summer after the caterpillar season is over.

Aphids also attract other insects, either to eat the aphids themselves or to eat the honeydew they secrete. Ants actually farm the aphids for their honeydew, sometimes moving them to better leaves or even to their nests. Hoverflies lay their eggs among the aphids and, when they hatch, the larvae eat the aphids.

So there are whole collections of creatures besides the aphids for the birds to feed on and in addition to the tits you may get wrens and dunnocks and various warblers snapping them up in high summer. Aphids are not unmitigatedly bad for the garden, either – it is thought that the sugar in their honeydew helps the soil when it drips into it.

Caterpillars on leaves are, as we have seen, another important food for birds – and blackbirds and thrushes may come and help remove the caterpillars of small white and large white butterflies from the cabbages in the vegetable patch. On the whole, though, you are not likely to want to plant flowers and bushes – let alone vegetables – just to attract insects. (Apart, that is, from bees and butterflies, which you may want not for the birds but for yourself! Buddleia is the best flower for butterflies, incidentally – sometimes dozens of red admirals, small tortoiseshells, peacocks and even painted ladies can be seen feeding on its nectar.)

Seeds

You may be more willing to let the birds have the seeds from your flowers. Many of the regular garden flowers will attract birds when they turn to seed. You can even set out to provide them with fresh sunflower seeds from your own tall blooms in the summer, besides buying sunflower hearts in packs!

Small flowers in beds and borders such as snapdragons, lavender, perennial cornflower, forget-me-nots and the rich purple-red honesty will have house sparrows and goldfinches coming for their seeds. You may even attract a shy, red-breasted bullfinch, and hear its soft note, like a very faint trumpet-call, in the trees, as it waits for a good moment to fly down.

Ornamental thistles and teasels will be very inviting to goldfinches, who have more slender bills than other finches, specially adapted for prodding into wild thistleheads. The tall purple-blue spires of sage can draw flocks of greenfinches when the seed has formed in their dry bells.

Berries

But it is berries, above all, that will provide home-grown nourishment for birds in the garden, sometimes lasting well into the winter. There are numerous berry-bearing garden flowers and ornamental bushes that can be of considerable importance to birds.

In the flower beds, the fat hips that linger on some roses after flowering may attract finches. The blue-grey berries of flowering currant are attractive to everything from tits to blackbirds, as are the blue berries that succeed the yellow blooms among the prickly leaves of *Mahonia*, or the Oregon grape – the birds can cope with the prickles better than humans can. Oregon grapes were actually first introduced to this country from America to feed birds: they provided both shelter and food for pheasants in game coverts.

Cotoneasters are an excellent shrub to plant. There are two main kinds, the wall cotoneaster and the Himalayan cotoneaster, and both of them produce red berries that are extremely popular with birds. The wall cotoneaster is a low plant with pink flowers and scarlet berries that may linger on the little bush from September to February. The Himalayan cotoneaster is a large bush, up to twelve or fifteen feet high, with red-marked white flowers, and more orangey-red berries that can also stay on the bushes till late winter.

Not only do the sturdy birds such as blackbirds and thrushes and the stout-billed finches such as greenfinches and bullfinches come eagerly to them, but they are the favourite fruit in Britain of a much rarer bird, the waxwing. This is a beautiful bird with a pinkish body and striking swept-back crest, a blob of red like sealing-wax on each wing, and a black and yellow tail. In some winters, such as 2000–01, very large numbers of them come here from Scandinavia after they have eaten all the berries on the rowan trees there. They eat rowan berries here too, of course, but they often turn up on roundabouts or in supermarket car parks and even in quite small, suburban gardens where cotoneasters are loaded with berries. You cannot guarantee them but if you grow cotoneasters you have a chance.

Another bush with berries that attract birds is the pinkish-purple, sweet-smelling mezereon, which has poisonous red berries that at least blackbirds can eat. Blackbirds also eat the black berries on privet hedges.

Finally, among bushes to plant both for birds and for the sake of their attractive appearance, there are barberry or *Berberis*, with its bright orange-red berries that used to be used for making jelly, and pyracantha, which has scarlet or yellow berries, and grows well against walls. There are other wild, native berry bushes that can be grown effectively in a flower garden, but I shall come to these when I write about wild gardens full of natural plants that many people might like to have as a supplementary garden, perhaps at the end of the main garden or on another side of the house.

As for fruit for human consumption – redcurrants and black-currants, raspberries, strawberries and gooseberries – I shall mention these delicacies, which birds fall on with zest and delight, in the last chapter of this book.

Trees

Many larger trees that you may want in your garden for beauty or shade also produce edible fruit for birds. Most of these are actually native species, but I shall mention them here rather than when discussing wild gardens, since they are not wild in the sense that brambles and thistles are. I shall also defer mention of elder and hawthorn to the section on wild gardens.

Yew trees and holly trees are often decorative items in a garden. Both offer good fare for birds. Flocks of noisy greenfinches may be found darting in and out of the dark foliage of the yews when the sweet, fleshy, pink berries are ripe in September and October. The late broods of young greenfinches can build up their strength on them. The graveside yews are also why you often find greenfinches in church-yards.

Holly berries in winter are particularly favoured by the thrush family and, if you have a large, well-berried holly tree, you may find that a pair of mistle thrushes have taken it over and are trying to keep all the berries for themselves. There will be much loud, angry churring coming from it as they try to drive other birds away.

Holly trees offer another attraction, this time to blue tits. Sometimes you see puffy, yellowish-brown blisters on the leaves in early spring. These are the homes of holly leaf-miners, the larvae of a little black fly – and blue tits love to attack them and extract the fat larvae inside. It has been observed – perhaps not surprisingly – that the tits are most successful on leaves that are not too prickly.

Silver birches overhanging a lawn offer seeds from late summer right through the winter. The seeds hang together in small, fragile catkins, and goldfinches, redpolls and siskins all do acrobatics to get at them. Of course, they scatter many seeds on the ground too and they drop down to eat those, so an undisturbed flock will be constantly flying in and out of the tree. They are very skilful at extracting the tiny seed from the papery wing in which it is enclosed. Other species, such as house sparrows, sometimes try to eat the seeds on the twigs, but more often are content to pick them up under the tree.

If you have a pond, or a stream running through the garden, alder trees at the edge attract the same birds. The alder seeds grow in small cones that turn black as they ripen and the birds tease the seeds out of the cones. Again they will go down to the ground to pick up fallen seeds.

As for big trees of the kinds fairly commonly found in gardens, beeches are one of the most productive in some years, when the hairy nut cases open to shed masses of sweet, white-fleshed nuts on the dead leaves below. Blue tits will get at them before they fall and great tits when they are lying on the ground. But in some years the nut cases will hardly contain anything except flat brown commas, with no flesh in them at all.

Hornbeams are not so common in gardens, but their seeds, which hang in lantern-like clusters, are very popular with greenfinches, who tear them off while they are still on the twigs.

Ash trees have bunches of long, winged seeds, called 'keys', in the autumn, and these often stay on the tree throughout the winter. Bullfinches come to feed on them, sometimes in small flocks.

Acorns that have fallen from oak trees may bring a beautiful bird, the jay, into your garden in the autumn and winter. It is a fairly large, mainly pink bird, with a conspicuous white rump, and a little, dazzling blue patch on each wing. When you see the bird perched, this patch is not very conspicuous, but I have noticed that when you look down on a flying jay from an upstairs window, practically the whole wing seems a glittering blue. By contrast, its main note is a harsh scream. It is a shy bird that slips inconspicuously through the branches and you very often see nothing but its retreating white rump, but it will come down to the ground to pick up acorns and will also bury them for future use. Magpies also like acorns, and hide them in the same way.

Woodpigeons eat the young leaves of many trees in early spring, with small flocks often going from one tree to another. You often see them at the top of the spire-shaped Lombardy poplars. They are comic to watch, because they are always venturing out on thin twigs to get at a succulent shoot at the tip and tumbling off because are they such heavy birds.

Poplar trees are often the host to great balls of mistletoe in their higher boughs. Other trees that are favoured by this Christmas berry are apples and limes. The names of birds are often misleading, but the mistle thrush really does like the pearly mistletoe berries more than any other bird. Like all thrushes, it wipes its beak on a twig, with the action of an old fashioned knife-sharpener, after it has been feeding – and the seeds it leaves behind spring up to form new mistletoe balls in other branches.

Of course, virtually all trees have insects on them, whether as eggs, larvae or chrysalids, or in the fully-formed last stage of their lives, when many of them are winged, and at any time you may see insect-eating birds looking for those. The insects on conifers will attract goldcrests, which can even hang upside down on a pine needle while hunting. The seeds in larch cones may attract siskins, while spruce and fir cones might just lure an occasional crossbill in winter. These are big finches, the male red and the female green, with the upper and lower mandibles of their beaks crossed. They clamber over the branches like parrots and use their beaks to prise open the cones, scooping the seeds out with their tongues. Like waxwings, they flock into Britain from the continent in some winters and are a fine sight to find in a garden.

The Wild Garden

Some house owners acquire a wild garden in the easiest possible way. They just neglect it. Other people cultivate an artificial wild life garden, growing exclusively native plants and flowers, and cunningly planning it so that not only birds but also butterflies and moths and mammals such as hedgehogs, bats and voles thrive in it. That is a delightful project but goes beyond the compass of this book.

However, many people with fairly large gardens might like to have a wild corner. Here, wild flowers and bushes and trees can be left largely to themselves and will attract many birds to feed and nest there. But astute planting will make it a much better bird garden.

Wild foods

The dominant plants in a wild garden are likely to be brambles and thistles – and nothing could be better for birds. The use of brambles by nesting birds we shall come to in a moment, but the blackberries themselves will be the draw from late summer into the winter. Pick as many as you like for yourselves and there will always be some left behind.

Greenfinches and especially bullfinches like blackberries and will go on eating them even when they have dried up and the juice has gone.

Once on a cold winter's day I saw a cock bullfinch pecking at the single, withered berry that was left on a long, thorny, bramble stalk. Blackbirds and robins will also go into the bramble bushes for blackberries, and in the autumn, before they leave for warmer countries, solitary birds or families from the warbler tribe may come down for them – willow warblers, garden warblers, blackcaps and whitethroats, all of which feed mainly on insects but like ripe fruit in season.

There are many other wild fruits that all these birds will take. Honeysuckle is a great adornment to a wild garden – its soft, bluish-green leaves start opening early in the year, its sweet-scented flowers are white or pink when they open and turn orange when they are pollinated and it produces a fine crop of brilliant red berries that birds will eat. Its twining stems will climb up slim tree-trunks and plants, or snake along the ground. Wild roses, or dog roses, are beautiful June flowers, and the scarlet rose hips that follow them last well into the winter, slowly turning black on the spiny twigs.

Hips and haws go together in popular sayings, and some of the other berries that birds like grow on bushes or small trees. Haws – which are the crimson berries of the hawthorn – are gobbled up by the resident thrushes. Later in the year, the winter-visiting thrushes, the fieldfares and redwings, also come to the hawthorns in search of them.

Fieldfares are large thrushes with a grey head and rump, a fine chestnut-coloured back and a boldly spotted breast. They have a loud 'chack-chack' call which you hear in the sky as they fly in. Redwings are smaller birds, like song thrushes with a red flash under the wing and a conspicuous creamy eyestripe. They make an odd, nasal clucking, and

also have a thin note, which is heard at night from migrating flocks flying overhead.

Fortunately for these winter birds, the haws often remain on the twigs for some time after they arrive from the far north in October and November. The fieldfares can be found quarrelling with the redwings in the hawthorn bushes, with the smaller bird generally losing out.

The black rosettes of berries on the elder trees and bushes are softer and juicier than the haws and, besides the thrushes, the warblers will also come for them. The red berries of the rowan or mountain ash trees among the red leaves provide a fine show in autumn and are soon snapped up. Wild cherries and, especially in the north of England and Scotland, the delicate-looking bird cherry trees are also good for planting in a wild garden. Blackbirds will sprawl in ungainly fashion over the twigs to get at any of these.

Crab apples come in many forms. The old English crabs have little sour green apples, but there are also species and hybrids with red or yellow fruits, which can lie in abundance on the ground beneath the trees and attract all the thrush family, who peck wastefully at them.

After the brambles and other fruit-bearing plants, we turn to the thistles and other seeds. Gardeners – and farmers – do not normally like thistles. The thistledown flies through the air, carrying the seeds in all directions as the wind shifts about, while underground the roots spread sideways and throw up new shoots. That is why the common field thistle is also called the creeping thistle. The thorny, dry stems in winter are also very unpleasant to handle.

But goldfinches love thistles. In a neglected field where the plants have run riot, you can sometimes see scores of goldfinches sitting on the seedheads, bending forward and inserting their beaks to tease the seeds out. In the trees at the edge of the field, others sing their tinkling song.

So there is a case for having a patch of thistles in your private wilderness. The goldfinches will be around till well into the winter, feeding on the ground where the thistles have collapsed and scattered their seeds. Later in the winter, if it is very cold, the goldfinches may go off south to France or Spain.

No other birds are so well adapted to tackling thistleheads as goldfinches, who are attracted to teasel for the same reason. The prickly, egg-shaped heads of teasel are flushed with pinkish-purple flowers in July and August, and then the seeds develop at the heart of the prickles, but male goldfinches can sit there and get at them. The females find it harder because they have slightly shorter beaks – only about a millimetre shorter, but it makes all the difference. Charles Darwin noticed this 150 years ago.

Some other species, however, will get at thistle seeds when they are looser and just about to blow away on the thistledown. Linnets, which are not very commonly seen in gardens, may come for them at this time. Linnets are delightful birds, with a reckless, sweeping flight, and a constant twitter full of lazy, twanging notes. The males have a red forehead and a red chest.

Linnets will also come for sorrel in the long grass, and for the seeds of various farmland flowers – or weeds, as farmers would say – such as fat hen, mugwort and the yellow-flowered charlock, all of which might grow and spread at the open edge of a wild garden once introduced. Mugwort, which is a tall scented plant with numerous woolly orange flowers, would interest greenfinches and might even bring down passing redpolls.

Some plants that are likely to appear in any bit of untended grassland or waste place can be visited sometimes for their seeds by finches. These include buttercups, persicaria (also known as red-legs because of its red stems), stinging nettles and of course dandelions.

Other wild flowers to consider introducing are knapweed (or hardheads) – a kind of thistle without prickles – and burdock. Burdock is the large plant whose round seedheads are covered with tiny hooks, and are well known for the way they cling to trouser legs and dogs' coats in order to get themselves distributed. Sowthistles and groundsel, which have feathery tufts of seeds, are eaten by bullfinches, but in a different way from goldfinches. The bullfinches' beaks are short and rounded, and instead of plunging them in from above to extract the seeds, they bite the seedhead on the side and get the seeds out that way.

Not all these sources of seed are particularly beautiful at a glance, but I find that all of them become more attractive the more closely they are examined – and for many of our British birds they are the countryside's natural larder.

Natural nests

The other benefit a wild garden can bring to birds is nesting sites. But here I shall also consider bushes or hedges, such as hawthorn, that could equally well find a place in a formal or flower garden and provide nesting places for some birds there too.

You may have old oaks or other large trees in the garden that date from the time when it was still woodland. If so, there will probably be some holes in them – often in places where a branch came off close to the trunk, and the wood has rotted in the centre of the scar it left behind. These are the natural nesting places for blue, great and coal tits, and for nuthatches. Other holes may have been drilled by green or great spotted woodpeckers at some period and taken over by tits or starlings.

Green woodpeckers are mainly woodland birds and do not often nest in gardens, but you may hear their mellow, laughing calls in the distance and occasionally get a glimpse of them looping away through the air, their backs like a golden spot of light. Great spotted woodpeckers have in recent years become more regular garden birds, and if a pair of them should nest in a hole in one of your trees, you will hear the male drumming in spring. He hits a piece of dead wood very rapidly with his strong beak and the sound rings out like a loud whirring, or can be mistaken for a creaking branch. This is the 'song' of the great spotted woodpecker, attracting females and warning off males like the songs of other birds.

Great spotted woodpeckers have bold black and white plumage, and if you see one on a branch above your head you will be struck by another feature – a brilliant blood-red stain under the tail. The males also have some red on the back of the head. As has been noted, they may come down to the bird table – or even to feeders – for peanuts, or to nesting boxes to try to eat the chicks inside.

Another nester in tall trees is the mistle thrush, which builds a sturdy nest high in the top branches. The male sings in the treetops, too, even in high winds – a single wild phrase, which sounds out like a bugle call and then ends abruptly, only to be repeated a moment later. He starts singing in mid-winter and goes on till June, and is sometimes called the storm-cock.

However, it is the bushes and hedges that are the main nesting places for garden birds. Blackbirds, greenfinches and dunnocks sometimes nest in large brambles and in a fairly large wild garden you may get a blackcap nesting in them. Garden warblers are a faint possibility, but in spite of their name do not often come out of the woods to nest in gardens. Another possible warbler visitor is the willow warbler, which sings a pretty cadence in the birch tops and very often makes its domed nest in long grass at the foot of a bramble bush. But it too prefers birch woods and copses and spinneys, to gardens.

Hawthorn hedges are a major nesting site throughout the British countryside. In gardens, as elsewhere, you may find blackbirds, song thrushes, greenfinches, hedge sparrows and sometimes chaffinches nesting in them. They all like a dense part of the hedge where their nests are well concealed by the foliage, and often you have to look very closely to find them. When I was a schoolboy, a friend and I invented a proverb: 'This year's nests are never found till next'. Very frequently, when the leaves have come off the hedges, you see a broken-down old nest there that you never suspected. Sometimes it has one addled egg in it, still colourful. Other good nesting hedges are laurel and tall beech.

Hawthorn bushes and trees are also used by these birds for nesting, but not, I think, so often as hedges, because the foliage is not usually quite so dense in them. Elder trees and bushes are often too thin for concealment, but they may be occupied. Woodpigeons and collared doves can nest in the branches of quite small, loose-textured trees. They lay two white eggs, which you can often make out through the flimsy platforms of sticks that serves them for a nest.

Both the collared doves and the woodpigeons will be singing around your garden for most of the year if they nest there. The collared dove's 'coo-COO-coo' song has been mentioned. The woodpigeon's song is a deep, lazy cooing with a fixed form. I invented this version of it: 'Take TWO books with you, take TWO books with you – dolt!' The 'TWO' is an emphatic coo, and the 'dolt!' is a sharp note with which the phrase generally ends.

Chaffinches and goldfinches have special preferences for nest sites. Chaffinches particularly like the fork of a medium-sized tree, such as an apple or pear tree – either a fork where a branch leaves the trunk, or a fork between two large branches. Their neat little moss-and-lichen-covered nest can be surprisingly well camouflaged there. Goldfinches also like fruit trees and build a mossy nest lined with plant down and feathers out on a swaying bough among the leaves.

What you may see if birds nest in your trees and bushes

We have seen what the behaviour was of birds that come into the garden to feed and also what the breeding cycle was like among those species that nest in boxes. Now we can turn to the breeding behaviour of those birds that are most likely to nest in the vegetation in summer.

Finches

Chaffinches make known their intention to nest in the garden at the beginning of February, when the males start singing. 'The chaffinch sings on the orchard bough,' wrote the poet Robert Browning – though he was actually referring to April in the poem, 'Home Thoughts From Abroad'. The song is a merry little run of notes that get faster and faster and end in a flourish – 'chip-chip-chip-chip-cherp-cherp-cherp-cherp-chippy-cheeoo'. It has been wittily compared to a fast bowler running up to the wicket and swinging his arm over.

The cock chaffinch may well be the same bird who was in your garden the year before, since they are very faithful to their territories. But the territories are quite big so you are not likely to have more than one pair nesting. He will inspect the trees to make sure that there are some suitable forks in them, and before long a female will have joined him, and have been accepted as his mate. She will not necessarily be the mate he had the previous year, though she may be.

You will see her also inspecting the tree forks, and she will choose the nesting place. But they will not start building until late April – they are relatively late nesters, waiting for the caterpillars for their young, like the tits. The female will build the nest with the male keeping her company, but she alone will incubate, while he sings on the bough again.

Her four or five eggs are very pretty – pale blue, with reddish scribbles and scrawls on them. As with the birds in the boxes, an occasional careful look when she is off the nest may do no harm, but it is best to disturb her as little as possible – and especially important not to alarm the young birds when they are getting bigger, in case they leave the nest too soon. The male helps to feed the young, and about a month after the hen began sitting, they will be out in the garden – brown-breasted birds like their mother. But they will soon go off to the woods to feed and their parents will not nest again that year.

Greenfinches have a similar cycle. But they are more sociable birds, and you may get more than one nest, especially if you have tall hedges. About the time that the chaffinch starts singing, you also start hearing the wheezing call of the greenfinch – like a long, sucking kiss. The song comes a little later in the year. Greenfinches make a loud, rattling twitter all the year round, and the song is like a snatch of this, followed by a run of slightly more musical notes. Sometimes you hear it from a male flying fast overhead and swaying wildly from side to side, displaying himself both to his rivals and to his mate.

The female builds the nest – a more substantial affair than the chaffinch's, with a solid base of roots – but the male, as with the chaffinch, accompanies her. She sits on four to six eggs, pale blue with rather heavier, more purple blotches than the chaffinch's. Both parents feed the young, regurgitating a mixture of seeds and insects that they collect in their gullets. This means that they can stay away longer looking for food, and not waste time coming back too often to the nest. The young can hold out.

I once saw a greenfinch's nest in a laurel hedge with four young ones in it, all ready to fledge. It was a bit late in their lives to be looking at the nest, but my excuse was that I had only just found it, and did not know what was in it. But I was glad I saw it. I thought that these four plump green nestlings, packed tight together, were just like a box of glaciated fruits, lime flavour.

Greenfinches go on nesting all through the summer, bringing up two or even three broods. The fledglings tend to stay around the garden in the bushes, making all kinds of strange squeaking and squawking sounds as they call for food.

Goldfinch pairs divide up the labours of nesting and bringing up young in the same way as the greenfinches and chaffinches, though the male will feed the hen on the nest. Their eggs, four to six in number, are again pale blue with purple or red scratches and blotches. The young lack the colourful head plumage of their parents until they moult in the autumn, but they look very charming sitting in a line on a telephone wire. The parents nest two or three times in the course of the summer and you may have a male singing high in the trees as late as August, when most garden birds are silent.

Thrushes

Blackbirds are often the commonest garden birds and they stay around all the year. Even if you only have one singing in the garden in summer, on a wall or a low branch, you will probably be able to hear others not far away. The song always seems to me to hold the quintessence of summer evenings – a lazy, fluting song that seems to collapse at the end of each outburst as if the bird were too indolent to go on, then a moment later resumes again in its relaxed and beautiful way. They sing from early February to early July, which is when the gardens altogether begin to fall more silent.

They nest quite early in the year, sometimes starting in March, if it is mild, and build in hedges and bushes. They will also nest on the window ledges of sheds, in creepers, and sometimes in curious places such as on a wing or seat of a car or tractor that is in regular use. Some of these travelling blackbird nests have survived with the protection of the owners of the vehicle and launched their young on the world.

The female builds, making a large mud cup which she coats and lines with dry grass. She sits on four or five blue eggs, mottled with reddish brown, and will often sit very tight when people approach the nest. The young are brown, like their mother, but more spotty. The male helps to feed them in the nest and also takes complete care of them for a few weeks after they have left the nest if his mate is quick to build and lay again. Otherwise, the parents will sometimes divide the brood up between them.

The fledgling young are very shy at first, hiding under bushes and calling with cheeping sounds that slowly turn into sharper calls. After a week or two they will come out on to the lawn and you can see them begging from their parents, but also starting to feed themselves. About three weeks after leaving the nest, they are virtually independent.

Song thrushes nest in the same kinds of bush and hedge as blackbirds, and also in concealed hollows behind creepers and similar places. They sometimes begin in March or early April, when their nests are easily seen among the leafless twigs. Like blackbirds, they make a strong mud cup, but they do not line it, so the eggs lie on the bare mud surface. The female builds and incubates; she lays four or five bright blue eggs with just a few dark spots on them. Both parents join in feeding the young, which are like short-tailed versions of their parents when they leave the nest. The fledglings are even shyer than young blackbirds, peering out nervously from time time from under the shade of bushes and slipping away from the garden when they are a little older without ever coming out on the lawn. The parents very often nest again after they are gone.

Other birds

Of all the garden birds, the wren is the least likely to come to the bird table – though you never know what will happen. Most of their life is lived in the undergrowth and few people realise that they are the commonest bird in Britain. It is thought that are seven million pairs breeding here each year. Someone remarked once that if each pair has eight offspring still alive in July – which is possible – that means there are 70 million wrens in the country at that moment – far more wrens than people. 'What a nice thought,' he added. The next commonest bird, incidentally, is the chaffinch with well over five million pairs, and third comes the blackbird, with well over four million pairs.

You may not often see a wren, but if one lives anywhere near you, you will certainly hear it singing. I have already mentioned its loud, vibrant, passionate-sounding song and its habit of singing higher up in the trees in spring, which gives one the best chance of seeing it.

The male wren builds several nests, and you may find them in all sorts of places in the garden – in ivy, in cracks in tree-trunks and walls, above shed doors, in the bottom of a hedge where the dead leaves accumulate. They are easily recognised, being domed affairs roughly constructed out of leaves and grass and moss. They are called 'cock's nests', and the builder's mate chooses one for their nest, lines it with feathers, and lays in it about eight tiny eggs, either pure white or sprinkled with pink.

I say 'the builder's mate', but in fact the cock wren sometimes has two or three mates, each of which chooses one of the nests he has built. These females tend to nest one after the other, with a slight interval between them, and they do all the incubating, but when the eggs start hatching the male starts work again, helping to feed each brood in turn. So with some males, the figure of 'eight offspring in July' might be an understatement. A little party of young wrens in a hedge, all with their tails turned up, is a delightful spectacle. However, there is very heavy mortality among these tiny creatures long before any of them reach maturity.

Those other reticent birds, the dunnocks or hedge sparrows, live even more extraordinary private lives. In spring you see a great deal of excited chasing and wing-flicking going on among them, but they settle down into curious communities, each with a dominant pair and various subordinate males and females. The dominant male mates with the dominant female and the subordinate females, and the subordinate males help to feed the young of the subordinate females.

The nests, which are the centre of all this complex activity, are built by the females in bushes and hedges, and contain four or five of the most beautiful eggs laid by small British birds – pure bright blue, like a reflection of the sky.

Finally, I mentioned the blackcap as a possible breeder in the brambles in a distinctly wild part of the garden. If one takes up a territory there, you will hear some wonderful outbursts of rich, rambling song some time in April or early May, and if the trees are still fairly bare you will fairly easily see the little grey bird with its black skullcap flitting through the boughs. A female with an orange cap may join it after a week or two.

Both birds will help to build the neat little grass nest, which may be in a bramble bush, but could also be in some thick honeysuckle up against a trunk, or in a fork of twigs in a shrub. Both birds also sit on the four or five blotchy pink eggs and help to feed the young, which are like their mother. They are insect eaters in midsummer, but you may see them all still around eating your raspberries and blackcurrants as the days start to shorten.

They will leave for Africa in September – and if you find a blackcap on your bird table in the winter, it will not be one of your own home-grown family, but a visitor who bred in northern Europe, and has got no further south than your garden.

Away from the House

If you have a really large garden or piece of land, you may be able to attract other birds to it, especially if there are barns or outhouses. There are special nest boxes available for these birds.

Owls

There are three kinds of owl that might live around your house and be tempted into your garden or grounds. These are the tawny owl, the barn owl and the little owl.

The tawny owl is the one that goes 'tu-whit, tu-whoo'. It is a large bird and comes out at night to feed on rats and mice, small birds, and other creatures whom its large eyes and, above all, its sensitive ears can detect moving in the darkness. Its victims cannot hear it coming,

because it flies so quietly with its ultra-soft feathers.

Actually, its 'tu-whit, tu-whoo' call is not quite what it seems. Most often it is the female owl that is making the 'tu-whit' sound – which is really more like 'ke-wick' – and the male replying with the long, wavering, hooting that the poets have described as 'tu-whoo'.

Even in towns, where there are parks and gardens, you may hear them calling in the trees, or see one sitting on a high lamp-post in the dusk. They sit silently all day in thick ivy or in other concealed places, and they nest in deep holes and cracks in trees.

There is a special kind of nest box that will sometimes attract them, called a 'nesting tube' or 'chimney'. It is a long, square box, open at the top and closed at the bottom, and would not be difficult to make for oneself. It needs good wood that will not warp, and should be about eight inches square at the entrance and two-and-a-half or three feet deep. It is put fairly high up in a tree, with the entrance upwards, and is either fastened firmly on the upper side of a sloping bough, or strapped tightly underneath one. There should be holes in the bottom so that any rainwater will run out. Some dead leaves or suchlike inside it at the bottom may make it seem more homely to prospecting owls.

If you get a pair of tawny owls in it they will be busy early in the year, perhaps even starting to nest in February. They will not make any kind of nest at the bottom of the tube, but lay their three or four white eggs on the floor that you give them. Be very careful if you try to look in the nest. It is best never to try. One photographer had an eye scratched out by the female owl's claws.

When the downy young hatch, the female goes on brooding them for two or three weeks, while the male brings mice to the nest. When the nestlings get bigger, she goes out hunting as well, for they are very hungry by now, and they stay in the nest for over a month altogether. They are still very downy even when they leave the nest, and the parents continue to feed them for most of the summer.

If you have thick bushes or hedges, or dense creepers, in your garden, this is where the tawny owls may find some of their food, for that is the kind of place where small birds roost at night. Sparrows and blackbirds are often noisy at sunset, when they first go to roost, but once they have settled down they are usually very quiet and still. However, a tawny owl may pick up the slightest movement – and sweep into the bush to carry one off.

The barn owl is the one that makes blood-curdling screams in the middle of the night – omens of death, they were once thought to be. It is sometimes called the 'screech owl'. It haunts farms and farmland, and its white shape is seen flickering along the edge of fields as the sun goes down, or wheeling in the beam of car headlights in the darkness.

Its way of life is broadly similar to the tawny owl's, though its nocturnal prey consists mainly of voles and shrews. It hears them squeaking faintly as they run through the grass.

It particularly likes nesting on rafters and ledges in barns and other farm buildings, but its numbers have been badly hit by the disappearance from the countryside of many of those nesting sites. So if you live among farmland and can provide a good home for a pair, you may well be lucky enough to get them nesting. You will certainly be helping the barn owl population if you do.

Again, there are specially-made boxes available. They are really just large versions of the open-fronted box that was recommended for robins and spotted flycatchers. The barn owl box needs to be fixed firmly somewhere in the rafters of of a building that has an open door or open sides – or at least has got holes in the roof – so that the owls can get in and out freely. There are also available more elaborate tent-shaped boxes with an entrance hole, which can be fastened to the outside of a building.

The eggs are white and the nestlings are downy, like the tawny owl's, but with the nest exposed up in the rafters you have a better chance of seeing the young. You will know you have got them, because both the old and the young birds make loud and rather funny hissing and snoring noises at the nest. If you get a good view of the adults, you will be struck by their strange, flat, white faces, and also by their orange upperparts, since they look all white in flight.

The third owl is the least likely to come to a nest box – but it can happen. This is the little owl, which is more of a daytime bird than the other two. It is smaller, as its name indicates, and is quite often seen sitting on a field gate, looking rather cross. It is not a native British bird, but since it was introduced just over 100 years ago it has become quite common in the countryside, where its loud 'whee-oo' call carries a long way.

It nests in holes, like other owls, and the box that has been designed for it is a straightforward nest box like a tit's, but larger and with a much larger hole – about four and a half inches in diameter. It is fastened to a tree, such as a pollard willow by a stream.

If owls come into your garden, you may find their 'pellets' lying on the ground. Owls generally swallow their prey whole, bones, feathers and all. But they disgorge all this indigestible matter in little bullet-like objects that quickly dry and crumble. The tawny owl's pellets are generally grey when they are dry, while the barn owl's are usually black. Schoolchildren nowadays are sometimes set the task of trying to re-assemble a mouse's skeleton from the bones found in a set of pellets found under the same tree.

Kestrel

Kestrels are a species of falcon, but they do not pursue their prey rapidly through the sky, as the peregrine falcon or the hobby do. Rather, they hover over the fields, facing into the wind with flapping wings, and looking down to see what is moving in the grass. Then they drop on it. In recent years they have become a familiar sight at the edge of motorways, where there is plenty of undisturbed life in the verges and embankments.

They may be seen over gardens, but are not very likely to hover over them – although I have heard of one swooping down and picking up a rat in as busy a spot as a Central London street. They usually nest on ledges on cliffs or high buildings, or in old crows' nests, but they are short of nesting sites, like the owls, and boxes have been successful in attracting them.

If you have a reasonably large garden and are not too far from good hunting-grounds for them, you could try putting up a box, similar to the open-fronted one recommended for barn owls, high on a tree-trunk. The male kestrel will bring food when the eggs first hatch, then the female will take over, and you may see the downy young ones peering out of the nest.

Swallows, house martins and swifts

These are the wonder-flyers in the world of small birds, tirelessly sweeping through the air catching flying insects. Swallows often fly low over lakes, or around horses, sheep and golfers that kick up insects from the grass. House martins are birds of the middle air, and swifts fly high for much of the time. It is thought that swifts may even sleep on the wing. They all have noticeably forked tails, with long streamers in the case of the swallow.

Swallows, which are glossy blue above and white beneath, may once have nested in caves, but for centuries now they have brought up their families in little mud nests on the rafters of barns and neglected garages. I have also found their nests in bird-watching hides and bus shelters. But they, like the barn owl, have had a harder time finding suitable nesting places more recently and they too can be helped if you have some kind of outhouse in places where they are found, especially in farmland.

Ensure, as for the barn owl, that any place where they might nest always has an entrance for them – though swallows will sometimes be happy just with a broken window, for they are masters at shooting through a gap without faltering.

If it is a suitable building, there is no reason why they should not nest there naturally, but they can be attracted by a bowl-shaped nest made of cement or of plaster of Paris. It should be about five inches wide, and can be moulded round a ball. If brackets are also put in either side before the mixture hardens, these can be used to attach it to a wooden panel, which can then be nailed or screwed to an inside wall, preferably a little distance above head height. Ready-made nests of this kind can be bought from specialist manufacturers.

If swallows do occupy your barn, you will have them around all the summer, since they have two or three broods a year. Both parents will build the nest, lining it with feathers, and the male will sing his twittering song on the roof while his mate incubates the red-spotted eggs. Then both of the pair will be off catching insects and bringing them back in a pouch in their throat, which enables them to collect more on each trip. Even after the young have left the nest, they will come back to it to roost. They can be distinguished from their parents by the absence of streamers on their tails, but they can fly just as brilliantly, and will take food from their parents in mid-air. The families gather in twittering flocks on telephone wires before they leave in the autumn for South Africa.

House martins, which are close relatives of swallows, nest in colonies in mud nests that hang under the eaves of houses. They take us back closer to home again, but I mention them here for convenience. They can be encouraged to breed by the provision of constructions similar to those suggested for the swallow. However, the cement or plaster bowls need to be deeper, with just a small hole at the top, and given a roof by the overhanging eaves of your own roof. Again, ready-made models can be bought.

House martins, like swallows, have two or three broods and can be around the house into October. They are the latest summer migrants to leave. Young birds from an earlier brood sometimes help to feed their later brothers and sisters. If you have them nesting on your house, you will have to put up with noise outside your window and streaks of white on the wall below. But remember that Shakespeare said, in

Macbeth, that where 'the temple-haunting martlet' breeds, the air is sweeter.

Swifts have a similar way of life to swallows and house martins, but they are not closely related to them. You know they are back, usually at the beginning of May, because the males go screaming round the roofs of buildings, flying very fast and showing off their powers.

They also career through the sky on their narrow, curved-back wings when they are feeding, and will fly very long distances to look for aerial insects, when falling rain makes them scarce nearer home.

They normally make a nest of bits of dry grass and feathers under the roofs of tall houses and church towers, finding a way in through cracks under the tiles or the eaves. They pick up the nesting material on the wing and glue it together with their own saliva. They are yet another species that is finding it harder to discover suitable places to nest, since modern buildings have fewer of these holes and hollows in the roof. In some cities in Holland, a country that is very bird- and con-servation-minded, new buildings must have suitable places for swifts to occupy.

Swift boxes can sometimes help. They are oblong wooden or 'wood-crete' boxes, with a slot-shaped hole in the front towards the bottom, fastened under the eaves. Swifts may also use old house martin nests or boxes. If they adopt one, the swifts can shoot straight into it with per-fect aim.

They lay three white eggs. Both sexes incubate and feed the young, which have the capacity to wait a long time for their parents to return with food. The fledglings finally plunge out of the nest, instantly capa-ble of flying, when they are anything between five and eight weeks old – it takes longer for them to grow up in rainy summers. Every year they leave for the drier skies of Africa before their parents, who rest and feed for a little while before they go. By the end of August, the skies round the haunts of the swifts are silent again. Three or four months is enough for them in Britain.

CHAPTER EIGHT

Last Thoughts about Birds in the Garden

Birds can do damage in gardens. That is a fact that must be faced. House sparrows have an appalling habit – from the gardener's point of view – of coming down on a lawn where the first crocuses are opening and tearing the flowers to shreds. They seem to concentrate particularly on the yellow crocuses. But they have a reason for it. They are pulling out the stigma of each flower – the tip of the female organs, which collects the pollen – because it contains saffron, which is rich in Vitamin C.

Another early spring marauder is the bullfinch, which eats the young buds on fruit trees in gardens and orchards. They particularly like the blossom-buds of pears and plums.

In the late summer and autumn, most of the fruit in the garden becomes very attractive to birds, especially to blackbirds and song thrushes. Strawberries on the ground, gooseberries, blackcurrants and redcurrants on the bushes (though, oddly enough, not so much white currants) – all may draw down those raiders, as well as tits and finches. Cherries can quickly disappear and windfall apples be pecked once and left ruined.

The only thing to do is net the fruit as carefully as you can, and hope for the best. Or you can simply do as the Victorian poet Lord Tennyson did – or said he did – with the blackbird in his garden: welcome him, and invite him to take what he wanted, unlike the poet's neighbours with their guns.

> O blackbird! sing me something well:
> While all the neighbours shoot thee round,

he wrote.

> The espaliers and the standards all
> Are thine: the range of lawn and park:
> The unnetted black-hearts ripen dark,
> All thine, against the garden wall.

It was worth it, he thought, for the sake of having the blackbird's song in his garden. His only complaint was that, by the time the fruit was in season, the blackbird had stopped singing. 'Plenty corrupts the melody,' he reflected – though of course the real reason that the blackbird was not singing was that the breeding season was over and the bird had no use for songs any more.

It is worth remembering, also, that in the summer sunshine you may attract to your soft fruit warblers that you would not otherwise get in the garden: blackcaps, garden warblers, willow warblers, and even perhaps their young families, three or four of them sitting together on a twig.

Moreover, you can set in the reckoning against any fruit you lose – or any pods of garden peas – all the aphids and caterpillars that the birds have eaten while the flowers have come and gone and the fruit has been forming. Birds are the best pesticides.

Songs

Tennyson's delight in the blackbird's song illustrates one of the really great pleasures of having birds in the garden. There may be a lull in the music in late summer, but after that there is song again all the year round.

The robins resume their territories in the autumn, as we have noted, both the males and the females taking up their own piece of land – without bothering about estate agents and contracts – and they will sing all through the winter, even in the middle of the night if the garden is lit by a street-lamp. I am often told excitedly by people that they have heard a nightingale behind their house in December, but I am afraid that it is always a robin.

There is often a burst of great tit song as the days draw in in September. In November, in some years, a song thrush will start singing again from the top of a tree in the dawn. The clear notes ring out loudly, as the thrush makes an early claim to a nesting territory for next year, but if the weather turns harsher he will stop singing and it may be late January before you hear him again.

I love those mornings in late January and early February, because that is when spring song really begins, and every day I am listening out for the first blackbird and the first chaffinch. Suddenly, early one morning, perhaps lying in bed, I hear a softly crooned bar or two as the milk-float purrs by – the first blackbird. And slowly the chorus will swell until, by the middle of March, the air is full of languorous blackbird melody, in which people have heard anticipations of composers from Beethoven to Bix Beiderbecke.

Perhaps a couple of days later there suddenly sounds forth the first cheerful, rattling song of a chaffinch. Then the wrens, who have been singing occasionally in the winter, break into loud and frequent song; the greenfinches begin wheezing and stepping up their twitter; the starlings' songs grow richer; the collared doves start cooing madly.

In town gardens, where most of the birds are residents, not summer migrants, the peak of the chorus – which is at its height at dawn – is in late March or early April. In the country, where blackcaps and willow warblers, swallows and cuckoos, add their voices in or over or near the garden, the peak is at the end of April. By May, many birds are too busy feeding their young to sing very much. By the end of July, most of the garden birds are silent again.

It is interesting to keep a note of the first time and the last time you hear a species singing (or see a summer visitor), and comparing the dates from year to year.

The unexpected

You can never know what you are going to find birds doing. Back in the 1920s, some householder must have been very surprised when he noticed one morning that a blue tit on the doorstep was pecking at his milk bottle top and drinking the cream. Since those days the habit has spread widely and blue tits can often be found supplementing their diet in this way. They are indefatigable explorers and have also been seen pecking at wallpaper and books and many other surprising surfaces, hoping no doubt to find insects behind them. It is worth keeping an eye on the blue tits in your garden, and seeing what they are up to.

When I have written in *The Times* about some unusual bird behaviour that has been observed, I have almost always received letters from readers reporting that they have seen something similar. The appearance of long-tailed tits on bird tables, mentioned earlier, is an example. When I wrote about it, it quickly turned out that readers all over the country had recently noticed the same thing, but not necessarily thought that there was anything surprising about it. There is no doubt that gardeners and other private birdwatchers have a store of knowledge that ornithologists lack.

Again, when I mentioned a report of some starlings picking dead flies from the bumpers of cars – they had been killed when the car had hit them – many correspondents wrote to me with reports of similar experiences. One person had seen starlings doing the same thing on the front of diesel locomotives in Paddington station. Others had seen house sparrows and pied wagtails taking dead insects from mudflaps and windscreen wipers. John E. Moore in Swansea saw a sparrow jumping up to the rear bumper of a car. Did the owner drive very quickly in reverse? he wondered.

There had been a robin who picked up large flies that had crashed into some patio doors, dazzled by the reflection of the light. It moved fast and snapped them up while they were still stunned. One reader in Salisbury, Christopher Tunnard, saw a wren darting from spider's web to spider's web outside a window, 'stealing either whatever had been caught in the web, or the spider itself'.

Birds themselves are often reported attacking their own reflection in a window. They mistake it for an intruder in their territory. A friend in Somerset told me about a grey wagtail that lived by a stream at the foot of his garden. It took to perching on the roofs of the cars outside his house, then flying fiercely at its reflection in the wing-mirrors. It went up and down the cars doing this so regularly that the locals called it 'the traffic warden'.

One of my correspondents saw a crow gathering walnuts from a tree in his garden, then flying up and dropping them to break their shells. One of the oddest sights I have ever seen was a blackbird sun-bathing, stretched out on a warm garden path with his head resting on a small stone like a pillow. One could go on for a long time with such stories – and any user of this book will find that he or she will be able to add to them.

The magpie question

Magpies are the legendary villains of the countryside today. Some people detest them so much that they shoot them with air rifles, or trap them and hit them over the head. Yet they are undeniably beautiful birds, with their black feathers shot with green and purple lights, and engaging birds, too, with their bold and lively ways, sitting on the very tip of a tree to look around them.

The main reason that they are hated is that they eat eggs and young birds. I understand the feeling very well. If you have found a robin nesting behind a loose bit of bark on a tree at the end of your garden, and have watched the incubating bird with its beady eye and looked lovingly on the downy nestlings, it is a bitter sensation to get up one morning and find the nest ravaged and the chicks gone. You glance up, see a magpie cackling on the roof, and your blood boils.

Nevertheless, it is wrong to criticise the magpie. It is only following its nature in eating these living things – and all the other birds in your garden, the robin included, are doing the same. Nor is there a conservationist reason for hating the magpie's activities. Many people believe that the decline in the number of song birds in Britain is due largely to the magpie's activities. But investigations by the British Trust for Ornithology and the Royal Society for the Protection of Birds have shown that on the larger scale there is no connection between magpies and falling bird numbers.

That is no consolation, of course, when you have lost your young robins. And you have a perfect legal right to kill the killer. But I do not think that is an appropriate response. For myself, I think it is best to leave nature as it is – enjoy the robins for what they are, and the magpie for what it is, and let them work out their own problems.

Visual Aids

If your bird table is near a window, you will be able to see plenty of bird life on it at close quarters. But a pair of good field glasses can increase your enjoyment of the birds in your garden.

The glasses will not focus very well on the bird table itself if it is too close, for they only work with objects beyond a minimum distance. However, if you see a bird at the end of the garden, or are looking up at one in a tree, they can help you to see it much more clearly and vividly. I am so used to having a pair of field glasses hanging round my neck that I feel they are practically part of me.

You want a pair that gives good magnification and lets in plenty of light, but is not too heavy. Field glasses are described as '8 x 30' or '10 x 50'. The first figure is the magnification – it means you see the object eight or ten times larger. The second is a measure of the light let in. The higher the figure in each case, the heavier the glasses will be. So most birdwatchers use a pair something between the ranges of the figures I have just quoted. '8 x 42' is a popular size.

Telescopes are used by birdwatchers more and more, especially since they have become relatively lightweight. But they are not so useful in a garden, where most of the watching will be at fairly close quarters. They have magnifications of 30x or more, and are most useful for watching wading birds out on mudflats, or birds out at sea.

They also need to be held very steadily unless they are on a tripod or some such stand. However, there are models now that you can fasten to the open window of a car, so that you can watch birds at a distance without getting out of the seat. One of these could always be attached to the frame of a window looking out on a garden.

Another way of watching the birds in your garden at close quarters is to film them. It is now possible to buy nest boxes with an infra-red camera and a microphone fitted in the roof, which will relay both pictures and sound to your own television set. Roofed bird tables, fitted up in the same way, are also available.

Why watch birds?

Yes, why do we do it? It has been suggested that it is a modification of our primitive hunting instinct and there is probably some truth in that. For myself, however, it seems to have more to do with the nature of birds. I cannot even glance up and see a starling flying over without a slight lift of the heart. I love the independence of birds from man, and especially the freedom that their powers of flight give them.

Of course, they have learned to exploit what human beings can offer them. The very existence of many bird species depends on the survival of a man-made countryside. To feed them in the garden and provide nest sites for them, is to draw them into a still closer relationship with human beings.

Nevertheless, they go about their lives in their own way, caught up in their own concerns, dividing up the land that we call ours for their own purposes, utterly indifferent to our interests. And when I watch them, I seem in some way to live and fly with them, also freed from my other human preoccupations. I am happy to return to those – but meanwhile birds have lifted me briefly into another life. I like to go and see them in remote places, but I also want to have them around me all the time. Gardens, for me, would never be the same without them.

Some Useful
Information

Suppliers

BirdGuides Ltd, PO Box 471, Sheffield S36 4YA. (Freephone 0800 91 93 91. www.birdguides.com.) Superbird food, including Sunflower Banquet and mealworms. Also books, CD-ROMs, and online information service about sightings of uncommon birds.

CJWildBirdFoods Ltd, The Rea, Upton Magna, Shrewsbury, SY4 4UR. (Freephone 0800 731 2820. www.birdfood.co.uk.) A wide range of bird food, feeders and nest boxes. Free *Handbook of Garden Feeding*.

Haith's, Park Street, Cleethorpes, NE Lincs, DN35 7NF. (Freephone 0800 298 7054. www.haiths.com.) Bird food. Family firm established in 1937.

Garden Bird Supplies, Ltd, Wem, Shrewsbury, SY4 5BF (01939 232233. www.gardenbird.com). Bird food, feeders and bird tables. Free *Garden Bird Feeding Guide*.

Gardman Ltd, High Street, Moulton, Spalding, Lincolnshire PE12 6QD (01406 372237). Wide range of bird food, feeders, bird tables and nest boxes.

Wild Bird News (Jacobi Jayne & Co), Priority 1, Freepost 1155, Canterbury CT3 4BR (0800 072 0130. www.wildbirdnews.com). Bird food, feeders, nest boxes. Free magazine *Wild Bird News*.

Jamie Wood Products, Dept RSPB2, 1 Green Street, Old Town, Eastbourne, East Sussex, BN21 1QN (01323 727291. www.birdtables.com). Hand-made feeders, nest boxes (including specialist boxes), and bird tables; also birdwatching hides.

Meripac Ltd, 17 Beaufort Road, London W5 3EB (020 8997 6077. www.Meripac.com). Specialist bird tables, squirrel baffles and window feeders.

Easyview Birding Company, Overlaw, Kirkcudbright DG6 4RA (01557 500604. www. easyviewbirding.co.uk). Window feeders.

Natural Collection (orderline 0870 331 333. www.naturalcollection. com). Adapter for turning water bottle into bird feeder.

Birdcam, 7 Bellfield Drive, North Kessock, Inverness IV1 3XT (01463 731525. www.bird-cam.co.uk). Nest boxes and bird tables fitted with cameras.

Organisations

Royal Society for the Protection of Birds. Leading bird conservation organisation with over a million members. Owns many bird reserves throughout the UK and champions the cause of birds. Also a supplier of all birdwatching and bird care accessories, including its own bird food. Quarterly magazine *Birds* free to members. Information: RSPB, The Lodge, Sandy, Bedfordshire SG19 2DL (01767 680551.

www.rspb.org.uk). Bird supplies (catalogue available): 0870 606 6333. www.charitygifts.com.

British Trust for Ornithology. Leading bird research organisation, using its bird population studies to promote their conservation. Organises a Garden Bird Feeding Survey and Garden Bird Watch in which members of the public can take part. Bimonthly magazine *BTO News* free to members of the BTO. Information: BTO, The Nunnery, Thetford, Norfolk, IP24 2PU (01842 750050. www.bto.org).

Birdline. Telephone information service with news of rare bird sightings. 09068 700 222. Calls cost 60p per minute. (See BirdGuides Ltd above for similar online service).

Books

The Mitchell Beazley Birdwatchers' Guide. By Peter Hayman (Mitchell Beazley, with the RSPB, £7.99). A long-established, popular guide with very helpful illustrations of over 350 species, and easy to slip into the pocket.

Collins Bird Guide. By Killian Mullarney, Lars Svensson, Dan Zetterstrom and Peter J.Grant (HarperCollins, £24.99). A comprehensive guide for more ambitious birdwatchers, with identification details, and clear, diagrammatic pictures in accurate colours of 722 European species.

Index of Birds